OFFICIAL SQA PAST PAPERS
WITH ANSWERS

INTERMEDIATE 2

BIOLOGY
2006-2009

BrightRED
PUBLISHING

First exam published in 2006.

Published by Bright Red Publishing Ltd, 6 Stafford Street, Edinburgh EH3 7AU

tel: 0131 220 5804 fax: 0131 220 6710 info@brightredpublishing.co.uk www.brightredpublishing.co.uk

ISBN 978-1-84948-038-3

A CIP Catalogue record for this book is available from the British Library.

Bright Red Publishing is grateful to the copyright holders, as credited on the final page of the book, for permission to use their material.
Every effort has been made to trace the copyright holders and to obtain their permission for the use of copyright material.
Bright Red Publishing will be happy to receive information allowing us to rectify any error or omission in future editions.

2006

[BLANK PAGE]

FOR OFFICIAL USE

Total for
Sections B and C

X007/201

NATIONAL
QUALIFICATIONS
2006

TUESDAY, 23 MAY
9.00 AM – 11.00 AM

BIOLOGY
INTERMEDIATE 2

Fill in these boxes and read what is printed below.

Full name of centre

Town

Forename(s)

Surname

Date of birth
Day   Month   Year   Scottish candidate number   Number of seat

SECTION A (25 marks)

Instructions for completion of Section A are given on page two.

For this section of the examination you must use an HB pencil.

SECTIONS B AND C (75 marks)

1   (a)   All questions should be attempted.

     (b)   It should be noted that in **Section C** questions 1 and 2 each contain a choice.

2   The questions may be answered in any order but all answers are to be written in the spaces provided in this answer book, **and must be written clearly and legibly in ink**.

3   Additional space for answers will be found at the end of the book. If further space is required, supplementary sheets may be obtained from the invigilator and should be inserted inside the **front** cover of this book.

4   The numbers of questions must be clearly inserted with any answers written in the additional space.

5   Rough work, if any should be necessary, should be written in this book and then scored through when the fair copy has been written. If further space is required, a supplementary sheet for rough work may be obtained from the invigilator.

6   Before leaving the examination room you must give this book to the invigilator. If you do not, you may lose all the marks for this paper.

SCOTTISH
QUALIFICATIONS
AUTHORITY
©

Read carefully

1   Check that the answer sheet provided is for **Biology Intermediate 2 (Section A)**.

2   For this section of the examination you must use an **HB pencil** and, where necessary, an eraser.

3   Check that the answer sheet you have been given has **your name**, **date of birth**, **SCN** (Scottish Candidate Number) and **Centre Name** printed on it.

    Do not change any of these details.

4   If any of this information is wrong, tell the Invigilator immediately.

5   If this information is correct, **print** your name and seat number in the boxes provided.

6   The answer to each question is **either** A, B, C or D. Decide what your answer is, then, using your pencil, put a horizontal line in the space provided (see sample question below).

7   There is **only one correct** answer to each question.

8   Any rough working should be done on the question paper or the rough working sheet, **not** on your answer sheet.

9   At the end of the exam, put the **answer sheet for Section A inside the front cover of this answer book**.

Sample Question

Which substances are normally excreted in urine?

A   Urea and salts

B   Protein and urea

C   Glucose and salts

D   Protein and salts

The correct answer is **A**—Urea and salts. The answer **A** has been clearly marked in **pencil** with a horizontal line (see below).

Changing an answer

If you decide to change your answer, carefully erase your first answer and using your pencil, fill in the answer you want. The answer below has been changed to **D**.

SECTION A

All questions in this Section should be attempted..

1. Which of the following prevents bursting of plant cells?

   A   Nucleus

   B   Cytoplasm

   C   Cell wall

   D   Cell membrane

2. Which of the following products is made using bacteria?

   A   Yoghurt

   B   Bread

   C   Beer

   D   Wine

3. Yeast respires anaerobically when there is a

   A   high concentration of alcohol

   B   low concentration of oxygen

   C   high concentration of carbon dioxide

   D   low concentration of sugar.

4. Respiration in yeast was investigated using the apparatus shown below.

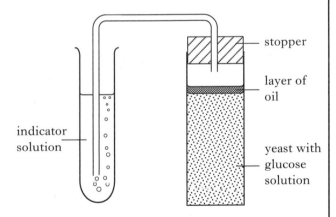

   Which of the following changes to the investigation would cause the yeast to respire more slowly?

   A   Use cotton wool instead of a stopper

   B   Do not add oil to the boiling tube

   C   Change the indicator solution

   D   Mix the yeast with water instead of glucose solution

5. The bar chart below shows the number of cells of different lengths in a sample of onion epidermis.

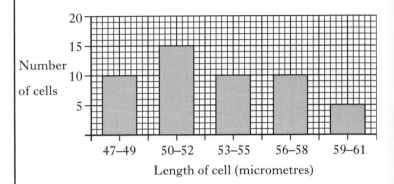

   The percentage of cells with a length greater than 55 micrometres is

   A   10%

   B   15%

   C   20%

   D   30%.

6. All enzymes are composed of

   A   carbohydrates

   B   protein

   C   glycerol

   D   fatty acids.

[Turn over

7. Two grams of fresh liver was added to hydrogen peroxide at different pH values.

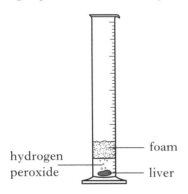

hydrogen peroxide — foam

liver

The time taken to collect $10\,cm^3$ of oxygen foam was noted for each pH.

pH of hydrogen peroxide solution	Time to collect $10\,cm^3$ of oxygen foam (s)
5	120
7	30
9	50
11	85

At pH 7, the enzyme which breaks down hydrogen peroxide is

A   at its optimum activity

B   at its minimum activity

C   denatured

D   digested.

8. The enzyme phosphorylase was added to a 2% glucose-1-phosphate solution. After one hour, the concentration of glucose-1-phosphate had fallen to 0·05%.

How many times lower was the concentration after one hour than at the start?

A   0·1

B   1·95

C   40

D   97·5

9. The table below shows the rate of photosynthesis by a plant measured at different light intensities.

Light intensity (kilolux)	Rate of photosynthesis (units)
10	2
20	27
30	51
40	73
50	82

What change in light intensity produces the greatest increase in the rate of photosynthesis?

An increase in light intensity from

A   10 to 20 kilolux

B   20 to 30 kilolux

C   30 to 40 kilolux

D   40 to 50 kilolux.

10. The word equation for photosynthesis is

A   carbon dioxide + water → glucose + oxygen

B   oxygen + water → glucose + carbon dioxide

C   glucose + oxygen → carbon dioxide + water

D   carbon dioxide + oxygen → glucose + water.

11. The diagram below shows an investigation into photosynthesis.

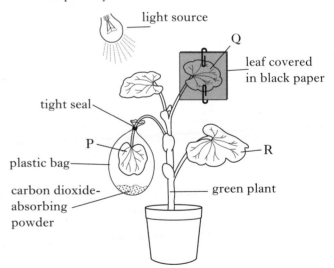

light source

Q

leaf covered in black paper

tight seal

P

plastic bag

carbon dioxide-absorbing powder

R

green plant

Which of the following statements is correct?

A   P, Q and R make food

B   only P and Q make food

C   only P makes food

D   only R makes food.

12. Plants compete mainly for

    A water, light and soil nutrients

    B water, food and soil nutrients

    C light, water and food

    D light, food and soil nutrients.

13. The total variety of all living things on Earth is described as

    A an ecosystem

    B biodiversity

    C a community

    D random assortment.

14. In Scotland, many forests are planted with a single species of tree such as Douglas fir.

    These forests have

    A a stable ecosystem

    B complex food webs

    C high intensity of grazing

    D low insect species diversity.

15. Which of the following sets of conditions are likely to cause woodlice to move about most rapidly?

    A Low humidity and low light intensity

    B Low humidity and bright light

    C High humidity and low light intensity

    D High humidity and bright light

16. A piece of potato weighs 20 g fresh and 5 g dry. What is the percentage water content of the potato?

    A 5%

    B 15%

    C 25%

    D 75%

17. The table shows water gained and lost by the body over a 24 hour period.

Method of water gain	Volume of water gained (cm^3)	Method of water loss	Volume of water lost (cm^3)
food	800	exhaled breath	300
drink	1000	sweating	
metabolic water	350	urine	1200
		faeces	100

What volume of water is lost by sweating?

A 150 cm^3

B 200 cm^3

C 550 cm^3

D 900 cm^3

18. Marine bony fish have to overcome an osmoregulation problem.

    Which line in the table describes how marine bony fish overcome this problem?

	Salts	Concentration of urine produced
A	absorbed	concentrated
B	excreted	dilute
C	excreted	concentrated
D	absorbed	dilute

19. Which of the following molecules is absorbed from waste food in the large intestine?

    A Glucose

    B Water

    C Amino acids

    D Glycerol

[Turn over

20. Bile is produced in the liver and stored in the gall bladder.

Bile is released into the small intestine where it

A digests fat

B digests glycogen

C emulsifies fat

D emulsifies glycogen.

21. From what substance is urea manufactured and where does this process take place?

A From amino acids in the liver

B From amino acids in the kidney

C From fats in the kidney

D From fats in the liver

22. The bar chart shows the volume of blood supplied per minute to the skeletal muscles and to other parts of the body of a healthy male at rest and during strenuous exercise.

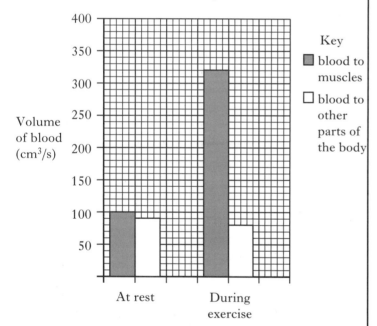

Key

▨ blood to muscles

▢ blood to other parts of the body

During **exercise**, the ratio of blood supplied to the muscles to blood supplied to other parts of the body is

A 1 : 4

B 4 : 1

C 10 : 8

D 10 : 9.

23. Which line of the table below identifies correctly the functions of macrophages and lymphocytes?

	Macrophages	Lymphocytes
A	produce antibodies	engulf bacteria
B	produce antibodies	produce antibodies
C	engulf bacteria	produce antibodies
D	engulf bacteria	engulf bacteria

24. The diagram below shows the neurones involved in a reflex arc.

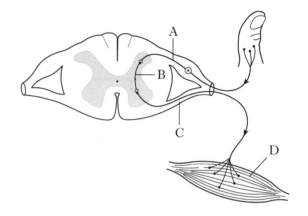

Which letter identifies the relay fibre?

25. Which of the following is a response to an increase in body temperature?

A Shivering

B Constriction of blood vessels

C Decrease in sweat production

D Dilation of blood vessels

Candidates are reminded that the answer sheet for Section A MUST be placed INSIDE the front cover of this answer book.

[Turn over for Section B on *Page eight*

SECTION B

All questions in this section should be attempted.
All answers must be written clearly and legibly in ink

Marks

1. (a) Decide if each of the following statements about the breathing system is **True** or **False**, and tick (✓) the appropriate box.

If the statement is false, write the correct word in the **Correction** box to replace the word underlined in the statement.

Statement	True	False	Correction
The trachea divides into two <u>bronchioles</u>.			
Air sacs are moist to allow <u>oxygen</u> to dissolve.			
Large numbers of <u>capillaries</u> surround the air sacs.			

3

(b) The following graphs show changes in lung pressure and volume during breathing in and breathing out.

Graph 1

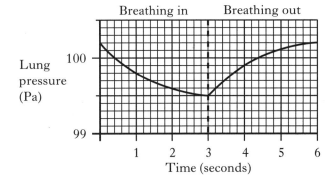

Graph 2

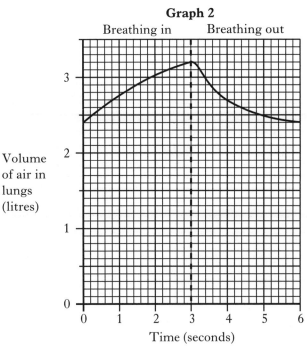

DO NOT WRITE IN THIS MARGIN

Marks

1. (*b*) continued

(i) From graph 2 calculate the volume of air breathed out in one breath.
Space for calculation

Volume = ________ litres **1**

(ii) State the relationship between lung pressure and the volume of the air in the lungs during breathing in.

____

____ **1**

(iii) What evidence from graph 2 supports the statement that the lungs are never completely empty of air?

____

____ **1**

[Turn over

DO NOT
WRITE I
THIS
MARGI

Marks

2. (a) The diagram below shows the heart and its valves.

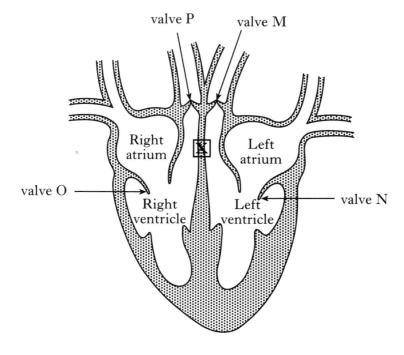

valve P   valve M

Right atrium   Left atrium

valve O   Right ventricle   Left ventricle   valve N

(i) What is the function of valves?

_____   1

(ii) Give the letters of the **two** valves which would open as blood leaves the heart.

_____ and _____   1

(iii) At birth some babies have a hole at point X as shown on the diagram. What effect would this hole have on the oxygen concentration of the blood circulating around a baby's body? Explain your answer.

Effect   _____   1

Explanation _____

_____   1

Marks

2. **(continued)**

(b) The diagram below shows part of the human circulatory system.

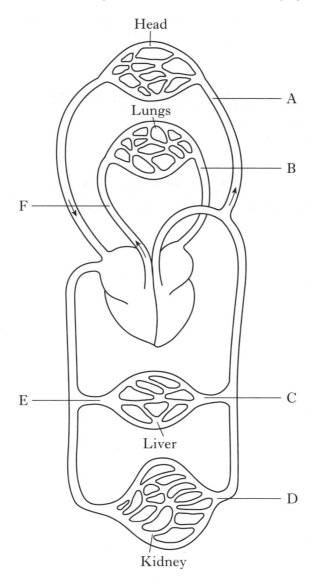

Head

Lungs

A

B

F

E

C

Liver

D

Kidney

(i) Use information from the diagram to complete the following table.

Name of blood vessel	Part labelled
Renal artery	
	B

1

(ii) Give **one** difference in the structure of arteries and veins.

_____

_____

1

Marks

3. (*a*)   Amylase is produced in the salivary glands. The substrate of amylase is starch. Amylase was added to a starch suspension and a sugar was produced.

(i)   Name the sugar produced by the action of amylase on starch.

_____   1

(ii)   State the optimum temperature for the action of amylase.

_____°C   1

(*b*)   An enzyme has a shape which is complementary to its substrate.

(i)   What term describes this property of an enzyme?

_____   1

(ii)   Name the part of the enzyme that is complementary to its substrate.

_____   1

Marks

4. (*a*) The bar graph below shows the energy content of equal masses of carbohydrate, fat and protein food types.

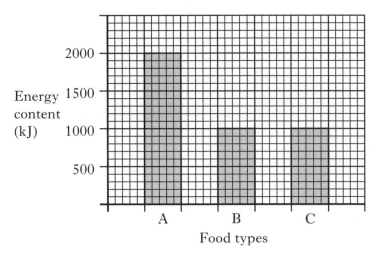

Identify food type A and give a reason for your answer.

Food type _____

Reason   _____   1

(*b*) Biuret reagent is used to identify protein.

State the colour of a positive result for this food test.

_____   1

(*c*) Name the element found in protein that is not present in carbohydrates and fats.

_____   1

(*d*) A healthy human diet contains a variety of minerals. Name one of these minerals and describe how it is used by the body.

Name _____

Description _____

_____   1

[Turn over

Marks

5. (*a*) The diagram below shows a plant cell and an animal cell.

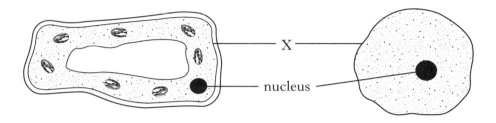

  (i) Identify structure X.

  _____   1

  (ii) Give a function of the nucleus.

  _____

  _____   1

(*b*) Three plant cells P, Q and R are shown below.

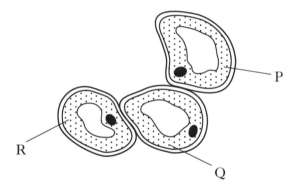

  (i) Cell P is hypotonic to cell Q and cell R is hypertonic to cell Q.

   Which cell has the highest water concentration?

   _____   1

  (ii) If all three cells were placed in pure water for one hour, what term would
   be used to describe the resulting appearance of the cells?

   _____   1

Marks

5. **(continued)**

(c) A biogas fuel generator is shown below.

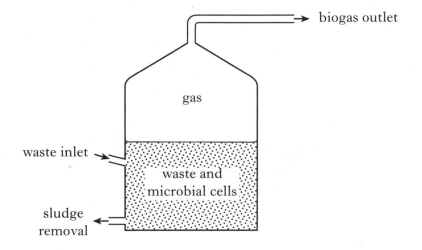

biogas outlet

gas

waste inlet

waste and
microbial cells

sludge
removal

(i) What type of microbial cells produce biogas?

_____   1

(ii) Name the main gas collected at the biogas outlet.

_____   1

[Turn over

Marks

6. The rates of photosynthesis and respiration in a green plant were measured over a period of 24 hours.

The results are shown in the graph below.

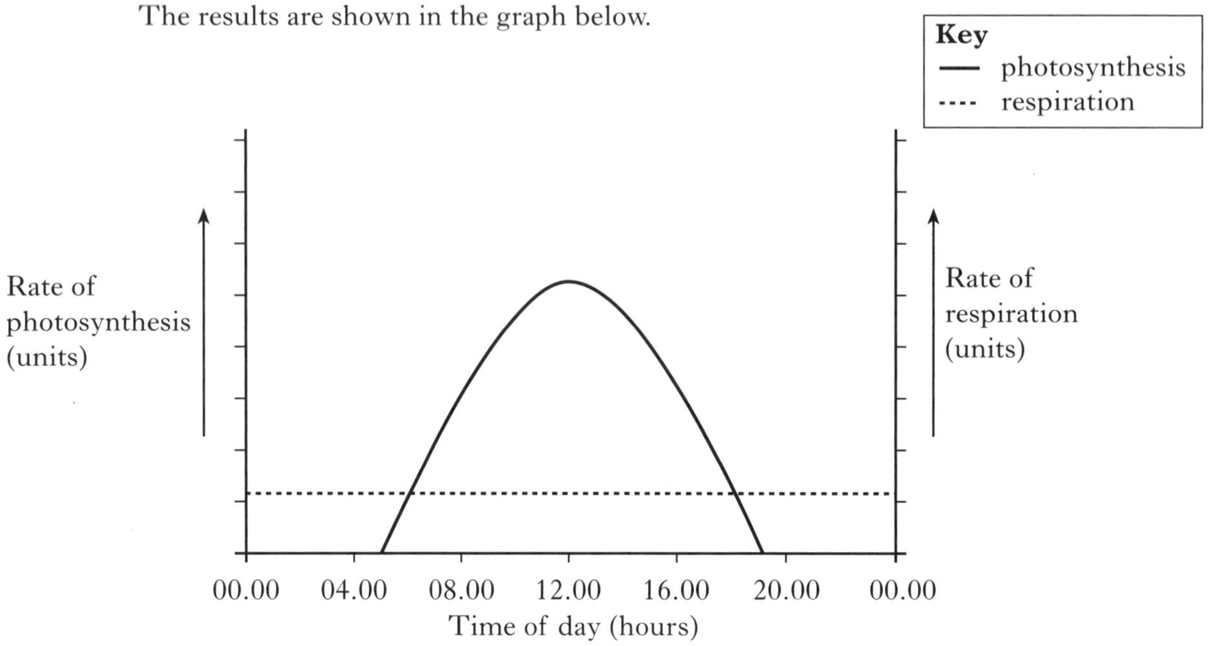

> **Key**
> —— photosynthesis
> ---- respiration

Rate of photosynthesis (units)

Rate of respiration (units)

00.00   04.00   08.00   12.00   16.00   20.00   00.00

Time of day (hours)

(*a*) (i)   At what time was the production of glucose at its maximum?

_____   1

(ii)   Between what two times was the plant producing more oxygen than it was using?

Between _____ and _____ hours   1

(*b*) What substance traps the light energy required for photosynthesis?

_____   1

Marks

6. **(continued)**

(*c*) The diagram below represents a summary of part of the process of photosynthesis.

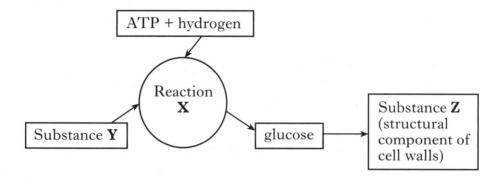

Name the following:

Reaction X _____

Substance Y _____

Substance Z _____   3

[Turn over

Marks

7. (a) The diagram below shows part of an investigation into the effect of adding three different concentrations of ATP solution to three pieces of muscle.

Equal volumes of the ATP solutions were added to the pieces of muscle.

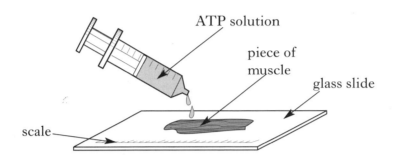

The results are shown in the following table.

Concentration of ATP solution (g per litre)	Length of muscle			
	At start (mm)	After 10 minutes (mm)	Decrease (mm)	Percentage decrease
1	35	34·3	0.7	2
5	50	46	4	8
10	40	33	7	

(i) Calculate the percentage decrease in length of the muscle with 10 g per litre ATP solution.

Complete the table.

Space for calculation

1

(ii) In this experiment why is it necessary to use percentage decrease in length in the comparison of the results?

_____

_____ 1

DO NOT WRITE IN THIS MARGIN

Marks

7. (*a*) (continued)

(iii) Explain why three different syringes should be used in this investigation.

____

____ **1**

(*b*) Muscle cells use energy for contraction.

State **one** other cell activity that uses energy.

____ **1**

[Turn over

Marks

8.   (a)   The diagram below shows a section of a river.

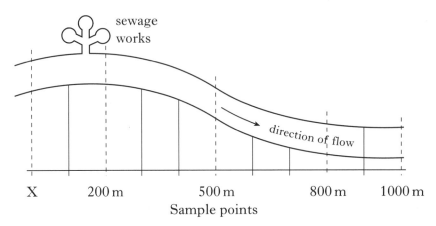

The table below shows the results of a survey into the oxygen content of the river at different sample points.

Distance of sample point from X (m)	Oxygen content (units)
0	1·20
200	0·04
500	0·20
800	0·40
1000	1·00

(i)   Construct a **line graph** of the results given in the table.

(Additional graph paper, if required, will be found on page 34)

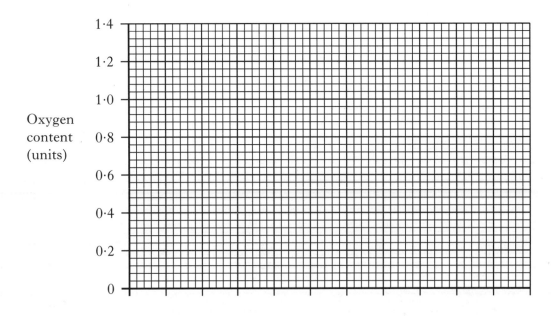

2

Marks

8. (*a*) (continued)

(ii) From the table calculate how many times greater the oxygen content is at 0 m than at 200 m.

Space for calculation

_____ times   1

(iii) Use data from the table to describe the relationship between oxygen content and distance of the sample point from X.

_____

_____

_____   2

(iv) The numbers of micro-organisms were counted at each sample point and found to be highest 200 m from X.

Account for the oxygen content of the river at 200 m.

_____

_____   1

(*b*) State the effect of an increase in pollution on species diversity.

_____   1

[Turn over

DO NOT
WRITE IN
THIS
MARGIN

Marks

9. (a) The diagram below shows part of a woodland food web.

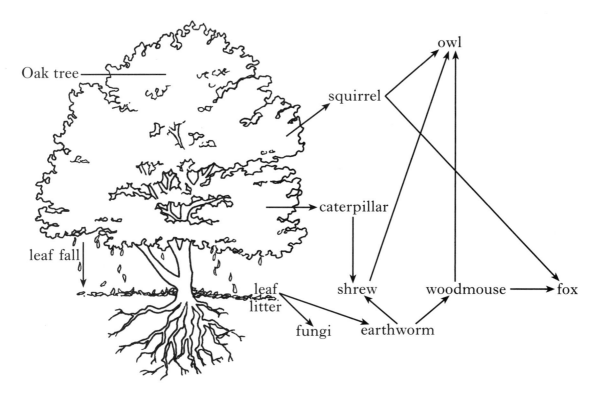

(i) Complete the table below using named examples from the woodland food web.

Type of organism	Named example
Producer	
Predator	
Decomposer	
Herbivore	

3

Marks

9. **(a)** **(continued)**

(ii)   The diagram below shows a **pyramid of numbers** taken from the food
web above. Suggest a food chain, from the woodland web, which would
give this pyramid.

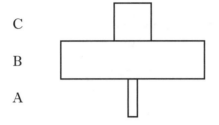

A _____ → B _____ → C _____   1

(iii)   Draw and label the pyramid of **biomass** for the following food chain.

leaf litter → earthworm → woodmouse → fox

1

(b)   State the term used to describe the role of an organism within an ecosystem.

_____   1

[Turn over

Marks

10. (*a*) Organisms vary from one generation to the next.
This variation may result from the following factors.

    A   Natural selection
    B   Selective breeding
    C   Environmental impact

Use this information to complete the table below.
(Each letter may be used once, more than once or not at all.)

Description	Factor
Produces changes not passed on to future generations	
Organisms that are better adapted to their surroundings survive and breed	
Effect of the surroundings on the final appearance of offspring	
Desirable characteristics chosen to produce improved offspring	

2

(*b*) Arrange the following stages of genetic engineering in the correct order.
The first stage has been given.

Stage number	Description of stage
1	Bacterial cell produces insulin
2	Insulin gene inserted into plasmid
3	Plasmid removed from bacterial cell
4	Plasmid inserted into bacterial cell
5	Insulin gene removed from human chromosome

Stage __5__ → ____ → ____ → ____ → ____

1

(*c*) Give **one** advantage of genetic engineering.

_____

_____

1

Marks

10.   (continued)

(*d*)   The desert plant shown below has adaptations to survive in dry conditions.

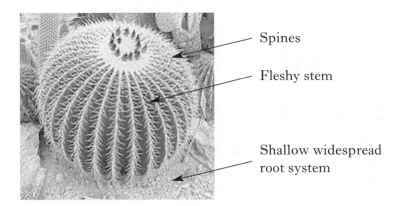

- Spines

- Fleshy stem

- Shallow widespread root system

From the diagram give **one** adaptation which reduces water loss.

_____   1

[Turn over

DO NOT
WRITE IN
THIS
MARGIN

Marks

11. In humans the length of the big toe is controlled by a single gene which has two alleles.

A father is homozygous for short big toe. A mother has long big toes. All of their children have short big toes.

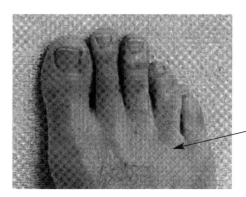

— Father's foot

(a) Complete the following sentences by **underlining** the correct word in each pair, using the information above.

$\left\{ \begin{array}{l} \text{Long} \\ \text{Short} \end{array} \right\}$ big toe is the dominant form of this gene.   1

The mother is $\left\{ \begin{array}{l} \text{homozygous} \\ \text{heterozygous} \end{array} \right\}$ and the children are all $\left\{ \begin{array}{l} \text{homozygous} \\ \text{heterozygous} \end{array} \right\}$.   1

Marks

11. (continued)

(b) The ability to roll the tongue is controlled by another gene in humans. The allele for tongue rolling (R) is dominant to the allele for non tongue rolling (r). The diagram below shows the occurrence of this tongue rolling gene.

Key

Female	Male	
○	□	tongue roller
⬤	◼	non tongue roller

mother   father

Kate   Jill   Ben   Jamie

(i) With respect to the tongue rolling gene, state Jamie's phenotype and Ben's genotype.

Jamie's phenotype; _____   1

Ben's genotype.   _____   1

(ii) Kate has a son and his father is homozygous dominant for the characteristic.

What is the percentage chance that the son is a tongue roller?

Space for working

_____%   1

(iii) State the two sex chromosomes present in Jill's body cells.

_____   1

[Turn over

Marks

12. (*a*)   The diagram below shows meiosis and fertilisation in humans.

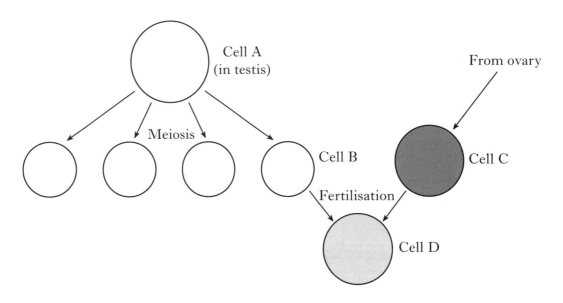

(i)   Complete the following table by naming the cells and stating the number of chromosomes present in each.

Cell	Name of cell	Number of chromosomes
A	testis cell	
B	sperm	
C		23
D		46

2

(ii)   Describe what happens during fertilisation.

_____

_____   1

(*b*)   (i)   Name a structure in a cell which is composed of a chain of DNA bases.

_____   1

(ii)   Explain the importance of the order of the DNA bases to the functioning of a cell.

_____

_____   1

[Turn over for SECTION C on *Page thirty*

SECTION C

Both questions in this section should be attempted.

Note that each question contains a choice.

Questions 1 and 2 should be attempted on the blank pages which follow. All answers must be written clearly and legibly in ink

Supplementary sheets, if required, may be obtained from the invigilator.

Marks

1. Answer **either** A **or** B.

    A.   The diagram below represents an animal cell that is respiring aerobically.

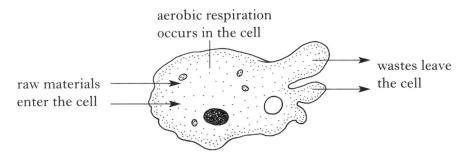

aerobic respiration
occurs in the cell

raw materials
enter the cell

wastes leave
the cell

       Describe the **two** stages of aerobic respiration. Include the names of the raw materials and the products of the two stages.

5

  OR

    B.   The diagram below represents an experiment set up as shown then left for 1 hour.

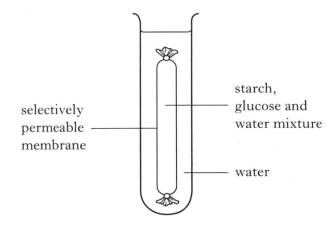

selectively
permeable
membrane

starch,
glucose and
water mixture

water

       Name and describe the **two** processes by which molecules would have moved.

5

Question 2 is on *Page thirty-two*.

SPACE FOR ANSWER TO QUESTION 1

**[Turn over for Question 2
on *Page thirty-two***

DO NOT WRITE IN THIS MARGIN

Marks

2. Answer **either** A **or** B.

Labelled diagrams may be included where appropriate.

A. Describe the role of the small intestine in the digestion and absorption of food. **5**

OR

B. Describe the roles of the hypothalamus and ADH in the control of the water concentration of the blood. **5**

[*END OF QUESTION PAPER*]

SPACE FOR ANSWER TO QUESTION 2

ADDITIONAL SPACE FOR ANSWERS

ADDITIONAL GRAPH PAPER FOR QUESTION 8(*a*)(i)

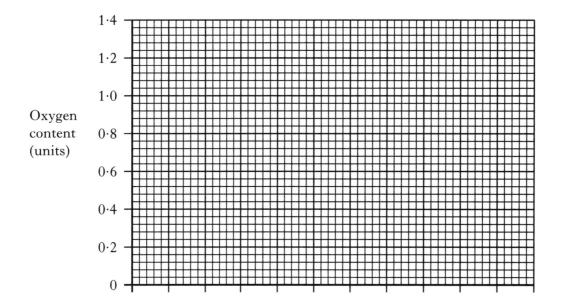

ADDITIONAL SPACE FOR ANSWERS

[BLANK PAGE]

[BLANK PAGE]

FOR OFFICIAL USE

Total for
Sections B and C

X007/201

NATIONAL
QUALIFICATIONS
2007

MONDAY, 21 MAY
9.00 AM – 11.00 AM

BIOLOGY
INTERMEDIATE 2

Fill in these boxes and read what is printed below.

Full name of centre

Town

Forename(s)

Surname

Date of birth
Day Month Year   Scottish candidate number   Number of seat

SECTION A (25 marks)

Instructions for completion of Section A are given on page two.

For this section of the examination you must use an HB pencil.

SECTIONS B AND C (75 marks)

1 (a) All questions should be attempted.

(b) It should be noted that in **Section C** questions 1 and 2 each contain a choice.

2 The questions may be answered in any order but all answers are to be written in the spaces provided in this answer book, **and must be written clearly and legibly in ink**.

3 Additional space for answers will be found at the end of the book. If further space is required, supplementary sheets may be obtained from the Invigilator and should be inserted inside the **front** cover of this book.

4 The numbers of questions must be clearly inserted with any answers written in the additional space.

5 Rough work, if any should be necessary, should be written in this book and then scored through when the fair copy has been written. If further space is required, a supplementary sheet for rough work may be obtained from the invigilator.

6 Before leaving the examination room you must give this book to the invigilator. If you do not, you may lose all the marks for this paper.

SCOTTISH
QUALIFICATIONS
AUTHORITY

Read carefully

1   Check that the answer sheet provided is for **Biology Intermediate 2 (Section A)**.

2   For this section of the examination you must use an **HB pencil** and, where necessary, an eraser.

3   Check that the answer sheet you have been given has **your name**, **date of birth**, **SCN** (Scottish Candidate Number) and **Centre Name** printed on it.

     Do not change any of these details.

4   If any of this information is wrong, tell the Invigilator immediately.

5   If this information is correct, **print** your name and seat number in the boxes provided.

6   The answer to each question is **either** A, B, C or D. Decide what your answer is, then, using your pencil, put a horizontal line in the space provided (see sample question below).

7   There is **only one correct** answer to each question.

8   Any rough working should be done on the question paper or the rough working sheet, **not** on your answer sheet.

9   At the end of the exam, put the **answer sheet for Section A inside the front cover of this answer book**.

Sample Question

Plants compete mainly for

A   water, light and soil nutrients

B   water, food and soil nutrients

C   light, water and food

D   light, food and soil nutrients.

The correct answer is **A**—water, light and soil nutrients. The answer **A** has been clearly marked in **pencil** with a horizontal line (see below).

Changing an answer

If you decide to change your answer, carefully erase your first answer and using your pencil, fill in the answer you want. The answer below has been changed to **D**.

SECTION A

All questions in this Section should be attempted.

1. Which structural feature is common to both plant and animal cells?

   A   Cell wall

   B   Chloroplast

   C   Nucleus

   D   Large central vacuole

2. Which line in the table below correctly matches the plant cell structure to its function?

	Plant cell structure	Function
A	Cytoplasm	Controls all the chemical activities
B	Cell wall	Keeps the cells turgid
C	Vacuole	Prevents the cell from bursting in a hypotonic solution
D	Cell membrane	Controls which molecules enter or leave the cell

3. Once yoghurt has been produced it is stored in a fridge.

   This is because

   A   bacterial growth is slowed down

   B   it makes the yoghurt more creamy

   C   it causes lactose to change to lactic acid

   D   the taste of the yoghurt is improved.

4. The diagram below shows the results of an investigation into the effect of different antibiotics on a type of bacterium.

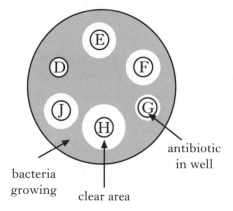

   Which of the following conclusions can be drawn from these results?

   A   These bacteria are resistant to antibiotic H.

   B   Antibiotic D is the most effective antibiotic against this type of bacterium.

   C   These bacteria are resistant to antibiotic D.

   D   This type of bacterium is resistant to all of the antibiotics.

5. The animals present in a sample of leaf litter were counted.

Animals	Number in sample
ground beetles	10
woodlice	35
slugs	5
centipedes	10
others	10

   What is the percentage of woodlice in the sample?

   A   35%

   B   50%

   C   65%

   D   70%

[Turn over

6. The diagram below shows energy transfer within a cell.

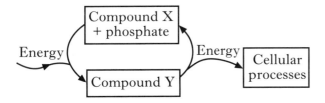

Which line of the table below identifies correctly compounds X and Y?

	X	Y
A	glucose	ATP
B	glucose	ADP
C	ADP	ATP
D	ATP	glucose

7. After running a race an athlete experienced muscle fatigue.

Which of the following had increased in the muscles?

A Glucose

B Oxygen

C ATP

D Lactic acid

8. Fermentation of sugar cane produces alcohol. What is produced when this alcohol is mixed with petrol?

A Biogas

B Gasohol

C Methane

D Carbon dioxide

9. Four cylinders of potato tissue were weighed and each was placed into a salt solution of different concentration.

The cylinders were reweighed after one hour. The results are shown in the following table.

Salt solution	Mass of potato cylinder (g)	
	Initial mass	Final mass
A	10·0	12·6
B	10·0	11·2
C	10·0	9·4
D	10·0	7·0

In which salt solution would most potato cells be plasmolysed?

10. An experiment was carried out to investigate the growth of pea plants kept in a high light intensity following germination.

The graph shows the average shoot length of the pea plants.

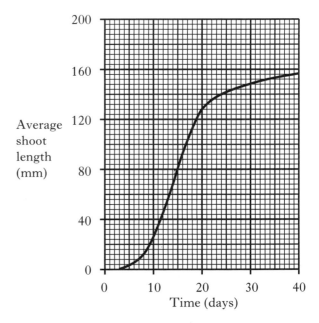

During which 5 day period is there the greatest increase in average shoot length?

A Day 10 – 15

B Day 15 – 20

C Day 20 – 25

D Day 25 – 30

11. The diagram below shows part of a food web in an oak woodland.

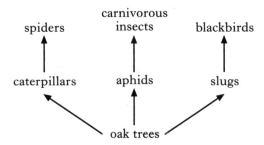

The use of insecticides in a nearby field resulted in the deaths of most aphids and caterpillars.

Which line in the table identifies correctly the effects on the numbers of slugs and carnivorous insects?

	Number of slugs	Number of carnivorous insects
A	increases	decreases
B	decreases	stays the same
C	decreases	increases
D	increases	stays the same

12. The diagram below shows a pyramid of biomass.

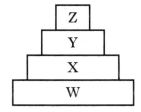

X represents the total mass of

A producers

B primary consumers

C predators

D secondary consumers.

13. Which of the following describes correctly a niche?

A The place where an organism lives

B Organisms and their environments

C A population of organisms in an ecosystem

D The role of an organism in an ecosystem

14. The table below shows the relationship between planting density and the mass of seed harvested for a cereal crop trial.

Planting density (number of plants per square metre)	Mass of seed harvested (grams per square metre)
4	60
8	86
15	105
32	77
128	21

What is the percentage increase in mass of seed harvested as planting density increases from 4 to 15 plants per square metre?

A 45%

B 75%

C 90%

D 105%

15. In humans, which of the following gametes are **not** normally formed?

A An egg with an X chromosome

B An egg with a Y chromosome

C A sperm with an X chromosome

D A sperm with a Y chromosome

16. The diagram below shows the same sections of matching chromosomes found in four fruit flies, A, B, C and D.

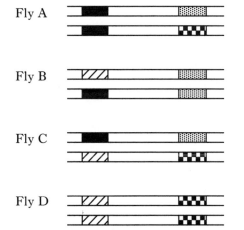

The genes shown on the chromosomes can be identified using the following key.

Key
- ▨ gene for striped body
- ▮ gene for unstriped body
- ▨ gene for normal antennae
- ▨ gene for abnormal antennae

Which fly is homozygous for both genes?

17. The diagram below shows a single villus from the small intestine.

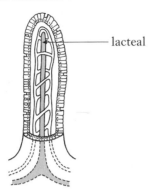

Which food molecules are absorbed into the lacteal?

A   Amino acids and glycerol

B   Glucose and amino acids

C   Fatty acids and glycerol

D   Amino acids and fatty acids

18. Which line in the table below describes correctly the changes in food due to digestion?

	Changes in food	
	Molecule size	*Solubility*
A	decreases	increases
B	decreases	decreases
C	increases	decreases
D	increases	increases

19. The diagram shows the apparatus used to investigate the energy content of fat.

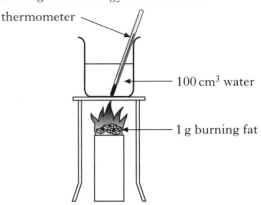

Which of the experiments shown below allows a valid comparison to be made between the energy content of fat and protein?

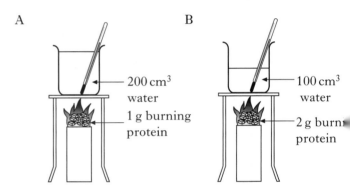

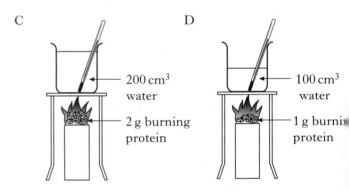

20. Bile is produced in the

A   liver

B   gall bladder

C   stomach

D   small intestine.

21. 100 g of baked beans contains 4·5 g of protein.

How many grams of beans would provide a daily protein requirement of 81 g?

A   5·5 g

B   18 g

C   364·5 g

D   1800 g

22. One way that marine bony fish cope with dehydration is

A   producing dilute urine

B   drinking seawater

C   producing large volumes of urine

D   absorbing salts.

23. The table below shows some features of blood vessels.

Which line describes features of veins?

	Direction of blood flow	Detection of pulse	Presence of valves
A	towards the heart	yes	no
B	away from the heart	no	yes
C	towards the heart	no	yes
D	away from the heart	yes	no

24. Which line in the table below identifies correctly how lymphocytes destroy bacteria?

	Phagocytosis	Antibody production
A	yes	yes
B	yes	no
C	no	yes
D	no	no

25. The graph below shows the relationship between the concentration of carbon dioxide and oxyhaemoglobin in the blood.

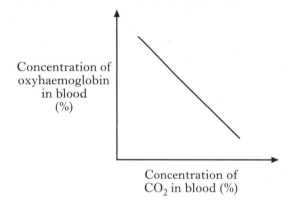

Which of the following describes this relationship?

A   As the carbon dioxide concentration decreases, the concentration of oxyhaemoglobin decreases.

B   As the carbon dioxide concentration increases, the concentration of oxyhaemoglobin decreases.

C   As the carbon dioxide concentration increases, the concentration of oxyhaemoglobin increases.

D   As the carbon dioxide concentration increases, it has no effect upon the concentration of oxyhaemoglobin.

Candidates are reminded that the answer sheet for Section A MUST be placed INSIDE the front cover of this answer book.

[Turn over

DO NOT
WRITE IN
THIS
MARGIN

SECTION B

Marks

All questions in this section should be attempted.
All answers must be written clearly and legibly in ink.

1. (a) The sentences below describe how oxygen enters the bloodstream for use in respiration.

   Underline one option in each set of brackets to make the sentences correct.

   Air entering the lungs passes down the $\begin{Bmatrix} \text{bronchioles} \\ \text{trachea} \end{Bmatrix}$ to the bronchi.   1

   To collect oxygen, blood enters the lungs through the pulmonary $\begin{Bmatrix} \text{artery} \\ \text{vein} \end{Bmatrix}$

   and returns to the $\begin{Bmatrix} \text{left} \\ \text{right} \end{Bmatrix}$ atrium of the heart.   1

   (b) The diagram below shows an alveolus in the lungs.

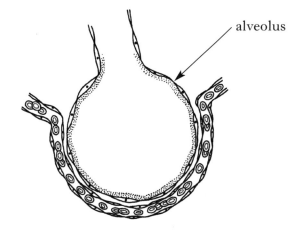

alveolus

   State **two** features of the alveolus that allow efficient gas exchange.

   Feature 1 _____   1

   Feature 2 _____   1

DO NOT WRITE IN THIS MARGIN

Marks

1. (continued)

(*c*) (i) Oxygen diffuses into muscle cells for respiration. Name **one** other raw material needed for respiration that enters by diffusion.

__________________________ **1**

(ii) Name a waste product of respiration that diffuses out of muscle cells.

__________________________ **1**

(*d*) Osmosis occurs in plant cells.

(i) Name the substance that enters or leaves cells by osmosis.

__________________________ **1**

(ii) What term describes the condition of plant cells after being placed in distilled water?

__________________________ **1**

[Turn over

Marks

2. (a) The experiment shown below was set up to demonstrate aerobic respiration in peas that are germinating (starting to grow).

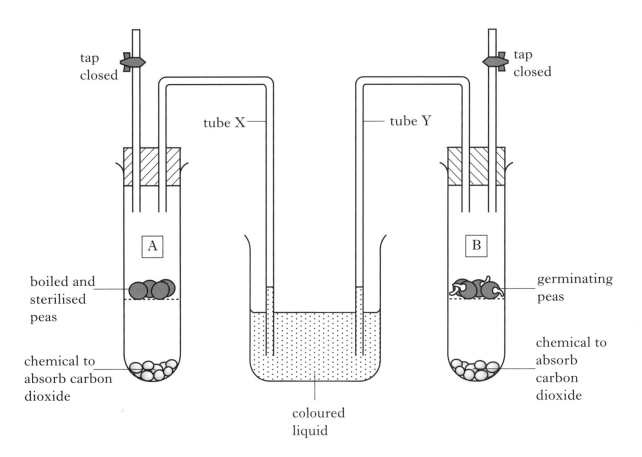

After two days, the level of liquid had risen in tube Y but had not risen in tube X.

(i) Explain the purpose of A as a control in this experiment.

_____

_____ 1

(ii) Predict the effect on the level of the liquid in tube Y if a greater mass of peas is used.

_____ 1

Marks

2. **(continued)**

(*b*) The following list contains some features of aerobic and anaerobic respiration in germinating peas.

List

W   Does not use oxygen
X   Produces carbon dioxide
Y   Yields 38 molecules of ATP per glucose molecule
Z   Produces ethanol

Complete the table below by writing the letters from the list in the correct columns.

Each letter may be used once or more than once.

Aerobic respiration in germinating peas	*Anaerobic respiration in germinating peas*

2

[Turn over

Marks

3. (*a*) A food sample was tested to find which food groups were present.

Both the Benedict's test and the Biuret test were positive.

(i) What colour indicates a positive result with the Benedict's test?

_____

1

(ii) Which food group was indicated by the Biuret test result?

_____

1

(*b*) Complete boxes 1 and 2 in the following diagram which shows information about the structures of three food groups.

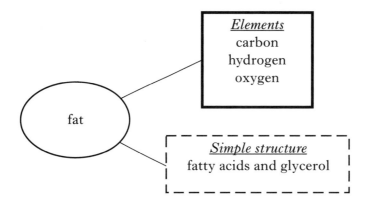

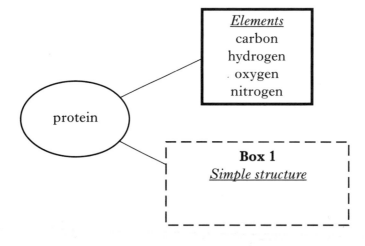

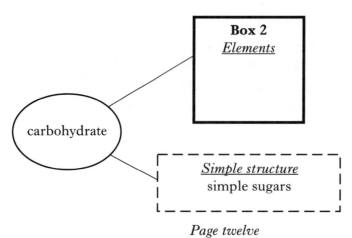

2

Marks

3. (continued)

(*c*) The graph below shows the results of an experiment into the activity of a stomach enzyme at various pH levels.

Mass of food undigested after 24 hours (grams)

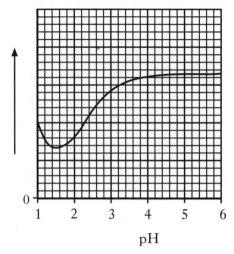

pH

(i) Name a stomach enzyme.

_____   **1**

(ii) From the graph, what is the optimum pH of this enzyme?

pH _____   **1**

[Turn over

Marks

4. (*a*) Four groups of students investigated the catalase concentration of different tissues.

Each group set up a test-tube containing 5 cm³ of hydrogen peroxide and a cube of potato. The oxygen was collected over a 3 minute period and the volume was measured as shown in the diagram below.

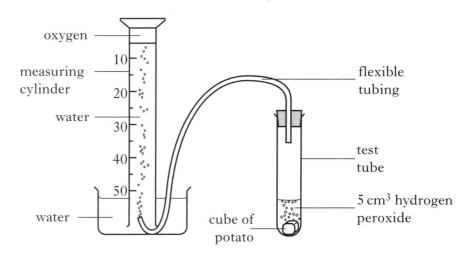

This procedure was repeated by each group using cubes of liver, apple and carrot.
The results from the four groups are given in the table below.

Tissue	Volume of oxygen collected in 3 minutes (cm³)				
	Group 1	Group 2	Group 3	Group 4	Average
Potato	5·5	5·0	5·5	6·0	
Liver	39·5	37·0	42·5	35·5	38·5
Apple	1·0	1·5	1·0	0·5	1·0
Carrot	3·5	3·0	3·5	2·0	3·0

(i) Complete the table to show the average volume of oxygen collected for potato tissue.

Space for calculation

1

(ii) The volume of hydrogen peroxide and time taken to collect the oxygen were kept constant in this investigation.

State **two** other variables that must be kept constant.

1 _____ 1

2 _____ 1

Marks

4. **(a)** **(continued)**

(iii)   What was done in this investigation to make the results reliable?

_____

_____   1

(iv)   What conclusion can be drawn from these results?

_____

_____   1

(b)   The diagram below shows the action of the enzyme phosphorylase in a potato cell.

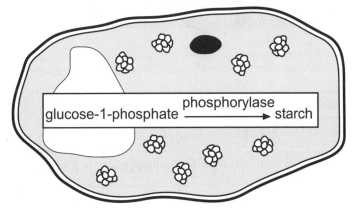

glucose-1-phosphate $\xrightarrow{\text{phosphorylase}}$ starch

(i)   <u>Underline</u> the option in the bracket to make the sentence correct.

The action of the enzyme phosphorylase catalyses the $\left\{ \begin{array}{c} \text{synthesis} \\ \text{degradation} \end{array} \right\}$ of

starch.   1

(ii)   State the effect of phosphorylase on the rate of this reaction.

_____   1

(iii)   Explain why lipase could not produce starch in this reaction.

_____

_____   1

[Turn over

Marks

5. (*a*) The diagram below shows the structure of the human urinary system.

Blood flow

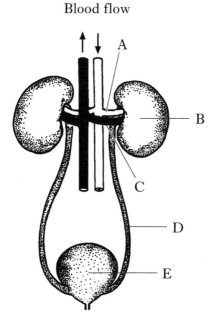

Complete the table to identify the structures and their functions.

Structure	Letter	Function
Bladder	E	
	A	Carries blood into the kidney
Ureter		Carries urine away from the kidney

2

(*b*) The diagram below represents filtration and reabsorption in the kidney.

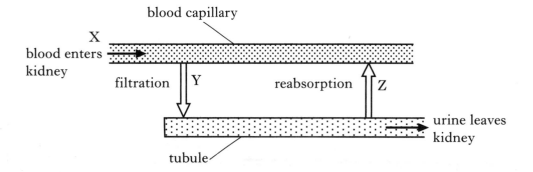

A hormone controls the volume of water reabsorbed at Z.

(i) Name this hormone.

_____

1

(ii) If there is a decrease in the level of this hormone, what will happen to the volume of water reabsorbed at Z?

_____

1

DO NOT WRITE IN THIS MARGIN

Marks

5. (*b*) (continued)

(iii) Tick (✓) the boxes in the table below to indicate which two blood components are filtered out of the blood at Y.

Blood components	*Filtered out at Y*
glucose	
salts	
blood cells	

1

(iv) The rate of flow at X, Y and Z is measured.

Rates of flow:

X = 1200 cm^3 per minute

Y = 125 cm^3 per minute

Z = 124 cm^3 per minute

How much urine will be produced in one hour?

Space for calculation

Volume of urine produced in one hour ____________ cm^3 **1**

[Turn over

Marks

6. The three types of neurone involved in the reflex arc for blinking are shown in the diagram below.

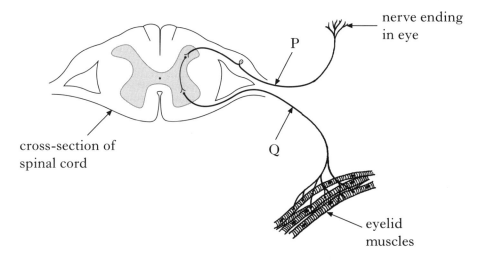

nerve ending
in eye

P

cross-section of
spinal cord

Q

eyelid
muscles

(a) Name neurones P and Q.

P _____

Q _____   2

(b) Which labelled structure is the effector in this response?

_____   1

(c) What is the function of a reflex action?

_____

_____   1

[Turn over for Question 7 on *Page twenty*

Marks

7. (a) An experiment was set up to measure the effect of light intensity on the rate of photosynthesis in the water plant, *Elodea*.
The light intensity was varied using a dimmer switch on the bulb.
The rate of photosynthesis was measured by counting the number of bubbles released per minute.

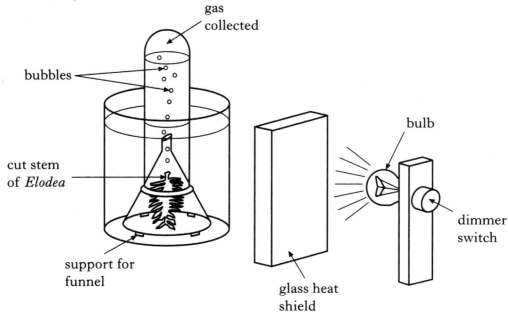

(i) Name the gas collected.

_____   1

(ii) The results of the experiment are shown in the table below.

Light intensity (units)	Rate of photosynthesis (number of bubbles per minute)
1	2
3	10
5	23
8	45
10	45
12	45

Marks

7. **(a) (ii) (continued)**

(A) On the grid below, plot a line graph to show rate of photosynthesis against light intensity.

(Additional graph paper, if required, will be found on page 32.)

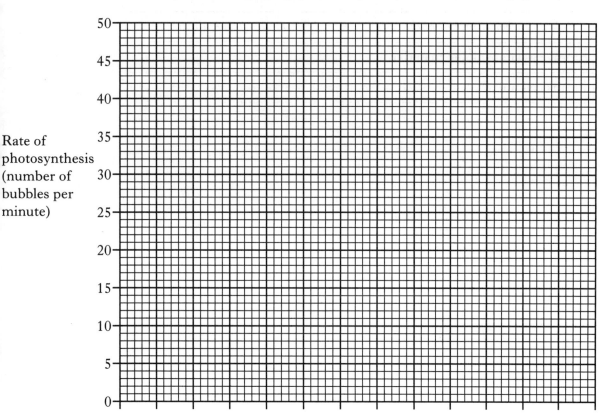

Rate of photosynthesis (number of bubbles per minute)

2

(B) Using the data in the table, explain the results obtained at light intensities greater than 8 units.

_____

_____   **1**

(b) There are **two** reactions in photosynthesis. The first reaction is photolysis.

(i) Name the two substances produced by photolysis that are required for the second reaction.

Substance 1 _____

Substance 2 _____   **2**

(ii) Name the second reaction.

_____   **1**

Marks

7. **(continued)**

   (*c*) Plant cells convert glucose into other carbohydrates.

   Complete the table below by naming two of these carbohydrates.

Role of carbohydrate in plant cells	Name of carbohydrate
Storage as an insoluble material	
Forms cell walls	

2

7. **(continued)**

Marks

8. (*a*) The diagram below shows a yeast cell.

(i) Name the structure shown in the yeast cell which contains the genetic information.

_____   1

(ii) A molecule consisting of chains of bases is contained in chromosomes.

(A) Name this molecule.

_____   1

(B) Explain how this molecule controls cell activities.

_____

_____

_____   2

(*b*) Gamete production is essential to sexual reproduction.

(i) Name the division of the nucleus that occurs during gamete production.

_____   1

(ii) Name the process occurring during this division that increases variation.

_____   1

(iii) Underline **one** option in each set of brackets to make the following sentences correct.

The number of chromosomes in gametes is $\left\{ \begin{array}{c} \text{half} \\ \text{twice} \end{array} \right\}$ the number found in

body cells.

The zygote is formed by $\left\{ \begin{array}{c} \text{fusion} \\ \text{division} \end{array} \right\}$ and contains $\left\{ \begin{array}{c} \text{half} \\ \text{twice} \end{array} \right\}$ the number of

chromosomes in a gamete.   2

Marks

9. In fowl, the dominant form (R) of one gene determines rose comb shape; single comb shape results from the recessive form (r) of the gene.

The diagram below shows the results of two crosses.

Cross 1 parents   True-breeding   True-breeding
                        rose comb fowl   single comb fowl

Cross 1 offspring   all rose comb fowl

Cross 2 parents   Rose comb fowl from   ×   Single comb fowl
                    Cross 1 offspring

Cross 2 offspring   Rose comb fowl   Single comb fowl

Ratio   1   :   1

(a) (i) Which offspring contains only one phenotype?

_____   1

(ii) Complete the Punnet square below to show the genotypes of the gametes of the Cross 2 single comb parent and the genotypes of the offspring produced.

	Genotypes of gametes of Cross 2 single comb parent	
Genotypes of gametes of Cross 2 rose comb parent R		
r		

2

Marks

9. **(continued)**

   (*b*) Decide if each of the following statements is **True** or **False**, and tick (✓) the appropriate box.

   If the statement is **False**, write the correct word in the **Correction** box to replace the word underlined in the statement.

Statement	True	False	Correction
A characteristic controlled by many genes is called co-dominant.			
The gene for comb shape has two different alleles.			
True breeding is another way of describing a homozygous individual.			

3

[Turn over

Marks

10. The small burrowing invertebrate, *Corophium*, is found in the mud of Scottish estuaries.

Corophium (magnified × 6)

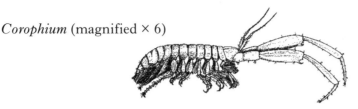

Corophium is the major prey of many species of migratory wading birds. These birds are present in large numbers from August to April.

The graph below shows the results of a one year survey on the numbers of *Corophium* taken on the first day of each month.

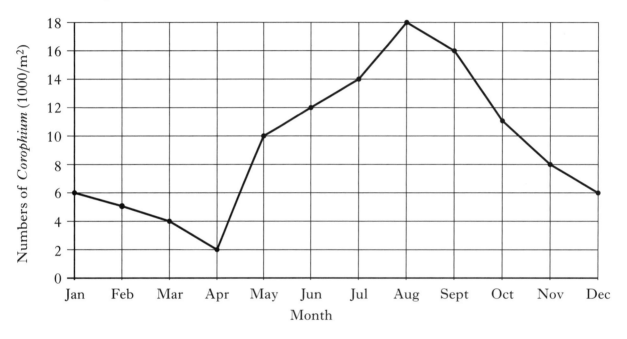

(a) Describe the changes in the numbers of *Corophium* from January to December.

_____

_____

_____   2

(b) How many times greater are the numbers of *Corophium* on 1st June compared to 1st April?

Space for calculation

_____ times   1

DO NOT
WRITE IN
THIS
MARGIN

Marks

10. **(continued)**

(*c*) Using all the information given, explain why there are high numbers of *Corophium* on 1st August.

_____

_____ **1**

(*d*) Predict what would happen to the biodiversity of this estuary if the wading birds stayed all year. Explain your answer.

Prediction _____ **1**

Explanation _____

_____ **1**

[Turn over for Section C on *page twenty-eight*

DO NOT
WRITE I
THIS
MARGI

Marks

SECTION C

Both questions in this section should be attempted.

Note that each question contains a choice.

**Questions 1 and 2 should be attempted on the blank pages which follow.
All answers must be written clearly and legibly in ink.**

Supplementary sheets, if required, may be obtained from the invigilator.

1. Answer **either** A **or** B.

    A. The diagram below shows human blood as seen through a microscope.

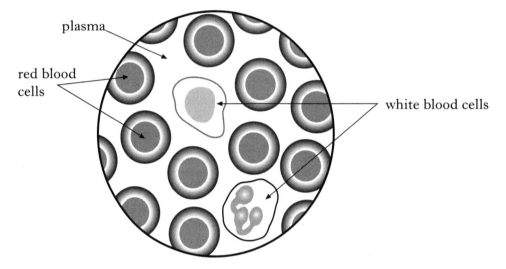

    (*a*) Name the **two** parts of the blood involved in the transport of substances around the body.

    (*b*) Describe how named substances are transported by each part of the blood.   **5**

    OR

    B. The diagram below shows a section through the brain.

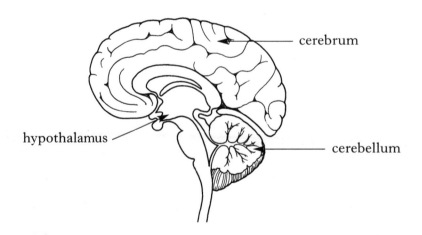

    (*a*) Name the part of the brain that regulates body temperature.

    (*b*) State its response to a **decrease** in body temperature by describing the changes which will occur in the skin, blood vessels and muscles.   **5**

    Question 2 is on *Page thirty*.

SPACE FOR ANSWER TO QUESTION 1

[Turn over for Question 2 on *Page thirty*

DO NOT
WRITE I
THIS
MARGI

Marks

2. Answer **either** A **or** B.

    Labelled diagrams may be included where appropriate.

    A. Genetic engineering uses bacteria to produce human insulin. Describe the
        stages involved in this process.   **5**

    OR

    B. Describe the process of natural selection as illustrated by the peppered moth
        Biston betularia.   **5**

[END OF QUESTION PAPER]

SPACE FOR ANSWER TO QUESTION 2

ADDITIONAL SPACE FOR ANSWERS

ADDITIONAL GRAPH PAPER FOR QUESTION 7(*a*)(ii)A

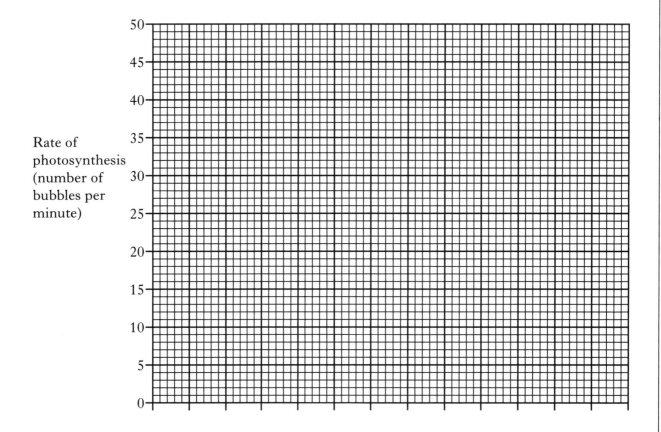

Rate of photosynthesis (number of bubbles per minute)

ADDITIONAL SPACE FOR ANSWERS

ADDITIONAL SPACE FOR ANSWERS

INTERMEDIATE 2

2008

[BLANK PAGE]

FOR OFFICIAL USE

Total for
Sections B and C

X007/201

NATIONAL
QUALIFICATIONS
2008

TUESDAY, 27 MAY
9.00 AM – 11.00 AM

BIOLOGY
INTERMEDIATE 2

Fill in these boxes and read what is printed below.

Full name of centre

Town

Forename(s)

Surname

Date of birth
Day Month Year   Scottish candidate number   Number of seat

SECTION A (25 marks)

Instructions for completion of Section A are given on page two.

For this section of the examination you must use an HB pencil.

SECTIONS B AND C (75 marks)

1   (a) All questions should be attempted.

(b) It should be noted that in **Section C** questions 1 and 2 each contain a choice.

2   The questions may be answered in any order but all answers are to be written in the spaces provided in this answer book, **and must be written clearly and legibly in ink**.

3   Additional space for answers will be found at the end of the book. If further space is required, supplementary sheets may be obtained from the invigilator and should be inserted inside the **front** cover of this book.

4   The numbers of questions must be clearly inserted with any answers written in the additional space.

5   Rough work, if any should be necessary, should be written in this book and then scored through when the fair copy has been written. If further space is required, a supplementary sheet for rough work may be obtained from the invigilator.

6   Before leaving the examination room you must give this book to the invigilator. If you do not, you may lose all the marks for this paper.

Read carefully

1 Check that the answer sheet provided is for **Biology Intermediate 2 (Section A)**.

2 For this section of the examination you must use an **HB pencil** and, where necessary, an eraser.

3 Check that the answer sheet you have been given has **your name**, **date of birth**, **SCN** (Scottish Candidate Number) and **Centre Name** printed on it.

   Do not change any of these details.

4 If any of this information is wrong, tell the Invigilator immediately.

5 If this information is correct, **print** your name and seat number in the boxes provided.

6 The answer to each question is **either** A, B, C or D. Decide what your answer is, then, using your pencil, put a horizontal line in the space provided (see sample question below).

7 There is **only one correct** answer to each question.

8 Any rough working should be done on the question paper or the rough working sheet, **not** on your answer sheet.

9 At the end of the exam, put the **answer sheet for Section A inside the front cover of this answer book**.

Sample Question

Plants compete mainly for

A water, light and soil nutrients

B water, food and soil nutrients

C light, water and food

D light, food and soil nutrients.

The correct answer is **A**—water, light and soil nutrients. The answer **A** has been clearly marked in **pencil** with a horizontal line (see below).

Changing an answer

If you decide to change your answer, carefully erase your first answer and using your pencil, fill in the answer you want. The answer below has been changed to **D**.

SECTION A

All questions in this Section should be attempted.

1. The diagrams below show four cells.

   Which cell is a leaf mesophyll cell?

   A

   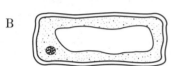

   B

   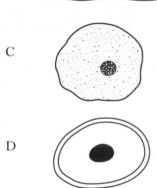

   C

   D

2. Which line in the table below identifies correctly the importance of diffusion to an animal cell?

	Raw material gained	Waste product removed
A	oxygen	glucose
B	carbon dioxide	oxygen
C	oxygen	carbon dioxide
D	glucose	oxygen

3. Which of the following molecules can both diffuse through a cell membrane?

   A Amino acids and starch

   B Amino acids and water

   C Starch and protein

   D Protein and water

4. Red blood cells burst when they are placed in water because

   A the cell contents are hypotonic to the water

   B the cell contents are isotonic to the water

   C the water is hypotonic to the cell contents

   D the water is hypertonic to the cell contents.

5. The energy yield per glucose molecule during aerobic respiration is

   A 2 molecules of ATP

   B 18 molecules of ATP

   C 36 molecules of ATP

   D 38 molecules of ATP.

6. The following are statements about respiration.

   1 ATP is produced

   2 Lactic acid is produced

   3 Carbon dioxide is produced

   4 Ethanol is produced

   Which of the statements are true of anaerobic respiration in human muscle tissue?

   A 2 only

   B 2 and 3 only

   C 1 and 2 only

   D 1, 3 and 4 only

7. The role of chlorophyll in photosynthesis is to trap

   A light energy for ATP production

   B chemical energy for ATP production

   C light energy for ADP production

   D chemical energy for ADP production.

8. The raw materials for photosynthesis are

   A carbon dioxide and water

   B oxygen and water

   C carbon dioxide and glucose

   D oxygen and glucose.

9. All proteins are composed of

   A genes

   B DNA

   C amino acids

   D bases.

10. Which of the following diagrams best represents the arrangement of chromosomes in a cell undergoing meiosis?

   A

   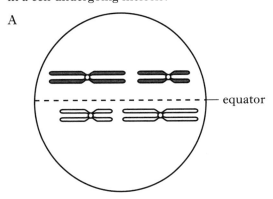

   equator

   B

   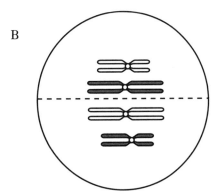

   C

   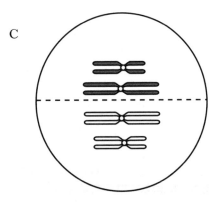

   D

   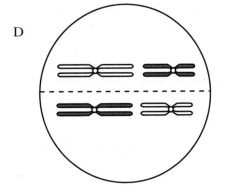

11. Which line in the table describes correctly the possible chromosome content of human gametes?

	Sperm		Ovum (egg)	
	Total number of chromosomes	Type of sex chromosome	Total number of chromosomes	Type of sex chromosome
A	23	X	23	Y
B	23	Y	23	X
C	46	X	46	Y
D	46	Y	46	X

12. In the fruit fly *Drosophila*, the allele for normal wings is dominant to the allele for short wings.

   A normal winged fly was crossed with a short winged fly and all the F_1 offspring had normal wings.

   If these F_1 offspring were to mate with each other, what percentage of the F_2 offspring would be expected to have normal wings?

   A 25%

   B 50%

   C 75%

   D 100%

13. The diagram below shows the same sections of matching chromosomes found in four fruit flies, A, B, C and D.

   Fly A

   Fly B

   Fly C

   Fly D

   The genes shown on the chromosomes can be identified using the following key.

   Key   ▨ dominant gene for striped body
           ■ recessive gene for unstriped body
           ▦ dominant gene for normal antennae
           ▧ recessive gene for abnormal antennae

   Which fly has a striped body and abnormal antennae?

14. In a breed of dog, the alleles for white coat colour and black coat colour are **co-dominant**.

A cross was performed between two heterozygous dogs.

Which line in the table below shows the numbers of different phenotypes and genotypes which are possible in the offspring?

	Number of phenotypes	Number of genotypes
A	1	3
B	2	3
C	3	2
D	3	3

15. Which of the following is an example of natural selection?

   A   Increased milk yield in dairy cattle

   B   Industrial melanism in Peppered Moths

   C   Insulin production by bacteria

   D   Insertion of DNA into a chromosome

16. The Peppered Moth is found in two distinct forms. One form is dark coloured and the other is light coloured. The moths rest on the trunks of trees.

   Pale coloured tree-trunks in an area were darkened by pollution. What would happen to the numbers of the two forms of the Peppered Moth in that area?

   A   The numbers of each form would increase.

   B   The dark form would increase and the light form decrease.

   C   The numbers of each form would decrease.

   D   The light form would increase and the dark form decrease.

17. Which of the following is **not** a benefit of selective breeding in crop plants?

   A   Higher yields can be produced.

   B   Undesirable features can be eliminated.

   C   Seed quality can be improved.

   D   Higher yields can always be guaranteed.

18. Lipase is an enzyme found in the small intestine. Lipase speeds up the breakdown of fat. Full cream milk contains a high proportion of fat.

Three test tubes were set up as shown in the diagram below.

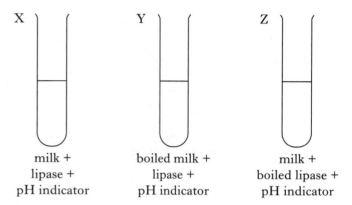

milk +
lipase +
pH indicator

boiled milk +
lipase +
pH indicator

milk +
boiled lipase +
pH indicator

The pH of the contents of each test tube was recorded at the start and again 15 minutes later.

What changes in pH took place?

   A   The pH decreased in each test tube.

   B   The pH increased in each test tube.

   C   The pH decreased in tubes X and Y and did not change in tube Z.

   D   The pH increased in tubes Y and Z and did not change in tube X.

[Turn over

19. The diagram below shows the apparatus used to investigate the energy contents of different foods.

1 g of each food was burned under a beaker containing $100\,cm^3$ of water. The rise in water temperature was measured using a thermometer.

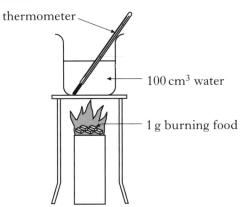

When different foods were burned, the following results were obtained.

Food	Temperature rise (°C)
potato	15
margarine	40
egg	20

The following equation can be used to calculate the energy value of food.

Energy value = 0·42 × temperature rise (°C) (kJ per gram)

Using this equation, the energy value of egg is

A   0·42

B   8·4

C   84

D   840.

20. The energy values of different food groups are shown in the table.

Food group	Energy value (kJ per gram)
Carbohydrate	19
Fat	38
Protein	19

What is the simple whole number ratio of the energy value in fat to protein to carbohydrate?

A   1 : 2 : 1

B   2 : 1 : 1

C   19 : 38 : 19

D   38 : 19 : 19

21. The following statements refer to the state of muscles in the gut.

Statement	State of muscles
1	contracted in front of food
2	relaxed in front of food
3	contracted behind food
4	relaxed behind food

Which statements describe peristalsis?

A   2 and 3

B   1 and 3

C   1 and 4

D   2 and 4

22. Tests were carried out on a sample of food. The result of each test is shown in the table below.

Food test	Iodine solution	Benedict's solution	Biuret solution	Translucent spot
Result	negative	negative	positive	negative

The sample of food contained

A   glucose

B   protein

C   starch

D   fat.

23. Carbon dioxide is removed from the body through the lungs. The correct pathway taken by a molecule of carbon dioxide out of the lungs is

A   alveoli → bronchioles → bronchi → trachea

B   trachea → bronchi → bronchioles → alveoli

C   alveoli → bronchi → bronchioles → trachea

D   trachea → bronchioles → bronchi → alveoli.

24. The graph shows the percentage saturation of haemoglobin at different oxygen concentrations.

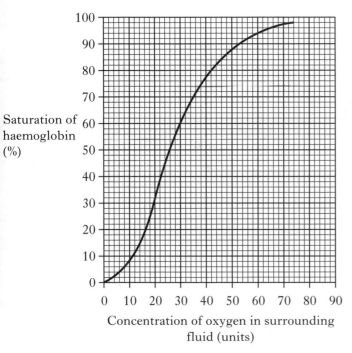

Saturation of haemoglobin (%)

Concentration of oxygen in surrounding fluid (units)

What is the percentage saturation of haemoglobin with oxygen when the oxygen concentration of the surroundings is 60 units?

A 30

B 90

C 92

D 94

25. The diagram below shows a side view of the human brain.

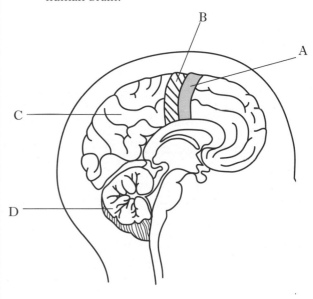

Which label identifies correctly the part of the brain which controls balance?

Candidates are reminded that the answer sheet for Section A MUST be placed INSIDE the front cover of this answer book.

[Turn over

[BLANK PAGE]

SECTION B

Marks

All questions in this section should be attempted.
All answers must be written clearly and legibly in ink.

1. (a) *Euglena* is a single celled organism.
   The diagram below shows some of the structures within *Euglena*.

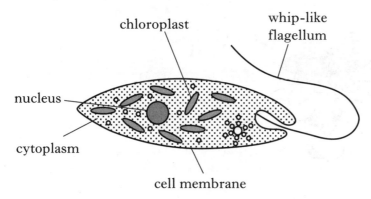

chloroplast

whip-like
flagellum

nucleus

cytoplasm

cell membrane

   (i) *Euglena* has structures found in most cells.

   Complete the table below to show the names of these structures and their functions.

Structure	Function
	controls the entry and exit of materials
Cytoplasm	
Nucleus	

2

   (ii) Name the structure that identifies *Euglena* as a plant cell.

   _____

1

   (b) Most plant cells have a cell wall.

   Name the structural carbohydrate in the cell wall.

   _____

1

[Turn over

Marks

2. Photosynthesis is the process by which green plants make glucose using energy from the sun.

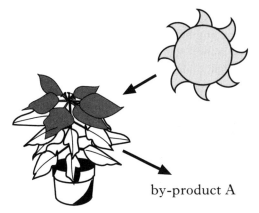

energy from the sun

by-product A

(a) Name the by-product A released during photosynthesis.

_____   **1**

(b) Hydrogen and a high energy molecule are produced during photolysis.

(i) Name the high energy molecule.

_____   **1**

(ii) Describe the use of hydrogen in carbon fixation.

_____   **1**

(c) (i) Explain why an increase in temperature can lead to an increase in the rate of photosynthesis.

_____

_____   **2**

(ii) Other than temperature, state **two** limiting factors of photosynthesis.

1. _____

2. _____   **1**

Marks

3. (*a*) The diagram below shows the link between aerobic respiration and protein synthesis.

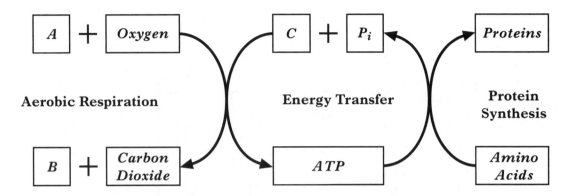

(i) Name substances A, B and C.

A _____

B _____

C _____   2

(ii) Some energy released in respiration can be used for protein synthesis. State one other cellular activity that uses energy.

_____   1

(*b*) The graph below shows lactic acid concentration in blood during a period of vigorous exercise (P) and of complete rest (Q).

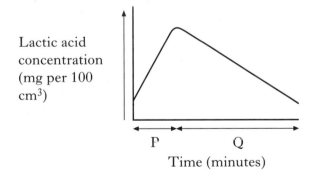

Explain why the lactic acid concentration changes during period Q.

_____

_____   1

[Turn over

Marks

4. A student cut five similar cylinders from the same potato, dried them with a paper towel and weighed them.

   Each cylinder was placed in a different concentration of sugar solution as shown in the diagram below:

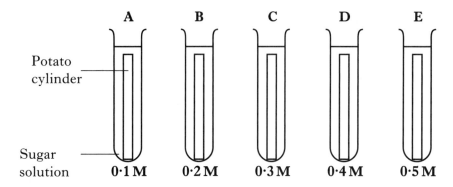

   After three hours, the student removed the cylinders from the solutions, dried and weighed them as before.

   The results are shown in the table below.

Test tube	Concentration of sugar solution (M)	Initial mass of potato cylinder (g)	Final mass of potato cylinder (g)	Change in mass of potato cylinder (g)	Percentage change in mass of potato
A	0·1	2·0	2·2	+0·2	+10
B	0·2	2·0	2·1	+0·1	+5
C	0·3	2·0	1·8	−0·2	−10
D	0·4	2·0	1·7	−0·3	
E	0·5	2·0	1·5	−0·5	−25

   (a) Complete the table by calculating the **percentage change in mass** of the potato cylinder in 0·4 M sugar solution.

   Space for calculation

1

   (b) (i) Name the variable altered in this investigation.

   _____   1

   (ii) Suggest one way in which the reliability of the results could be improved.

   _____   1

DO NOT WRITE IN THIS MARGIN

Marks

4. (*b*) (continued)

(iii) Would the results be valid if the cylinders were **not** dried before being weighed? Tick (✓) the correct box.

Valid ☐ Not valid ☐

Explain your answer.

Explanation ______________________________

____

______________________________ **1**

(*c*) (i) State the letter of one test tube containing a potato cylinder in a **hypertonic** solution.

Letter __________ **1**

(ii) Predict the appearance of the potato cylinder in test tube E after three hours.

______________________________ **1**

[Turn over

Marks

5. The pictures show some organisms from a marine ecosystem.

   The pictures are not to scale.

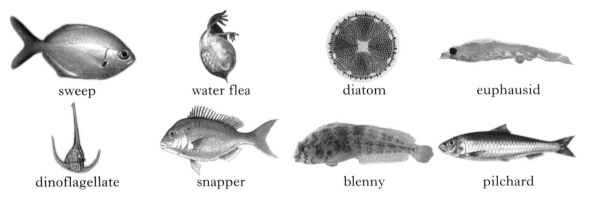

sweep	water flea	diatom	euphausid
dinoflagellate	snapper	blenny	pilchard

The table below shows information about the feeding relationships in the marine ecosystem.

Organism	Food eaten
euphasid	dinoflagellate, diatom
dinoflagellate	none
sweep	diatom
snapper	sweep, pilchard, blenny
pilchard	water flea, euphausid
blenny	water flea, euphausid
diatom	none
water flea	diatom, dinoflagellate

(a) (i) Use the information in the table to complete the food web below.

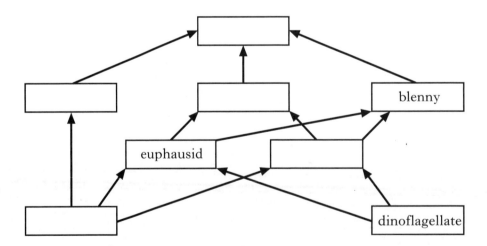

2

   (ii) What term is used to describe the snapper in this ecosystem?

   _____

1

DO NOT WRITE IN THIS MARGIN

Marks

5. (continued)

(*b*) A pod of dolphins arrived in the area. Dolphins feed on snappers.

Describe the effect of the dolphins on the size of the euphausid population. Explain your answer.

Effect ____________________ **1**

Explanation ____

____ **1**

[Turn over

Marks

6. The table shows the number of pilot whales caught in the Faroe islands between 1994 and 2000.

Year	Number of pilot whales caught
1994	1200
1995	228
1996	1500
1997	1170
1998	820
1999	610
2000	580

(a) (i) Construct a **bar graph** of the results given from **1996** to **2000**.

(Additional graph paper, if required, will be found on page 32)

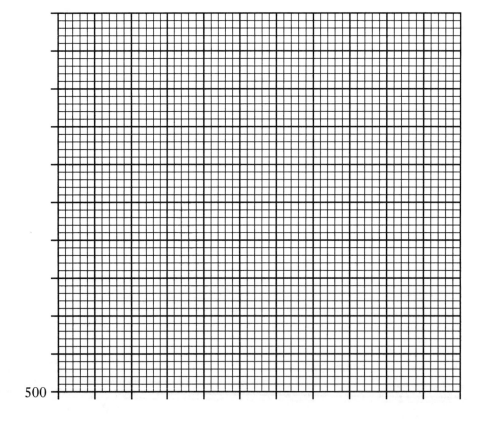

500

3

DO NOT WRITE IN THIS MARGIN

Marks

6. **(*a*) (continued)**

(ii) Describe the trend shown by the results in the table from **1996** to **2000**.

____

____ 1

(iii) What is the average yearly pilot whale catch from **1996** to **2000**?

Space for calculation

average ____________ 1

(*b*) How many times greater was the pilot whale catch in 1996 than in 1994?

Space for calculation

____________ times 1

[Turn over

Marks

7. Feather colour in parrots is controlled by a single gene. Blue feather colour (B) is dominant to yellow feather colour (b).

(a) A homozygous blue parrot is crossed with a homozygous yellow parrot.

(i) Complete the genotypes of the P generation.

P   phenotype   blue   X   yellow

P   genotype   ———————   ———————   1

(ii) State the genotype of the F_1 parrots.

F_1 genotype   ———————   1

(iii) State the phenotype of the F_1 parrots.

F_1 phenotype ———————   1

(b) An F_1 individual is crossed with a true breeding yellow parrot.

Complete the punnet square to show the expected results of this cross.

Genotype of gametes
from F_1 parent

Genotype of
gametes from
yellow parent

2

Marks

8. (*a*) In African grasslands impala, giraffe and zebra feed on *Acacia* trees. Impala and zebra also graze on grasses.

Acacia	impala	giraffe	zebra

(i) State one way that competition for food is reduced between zebras and giraffes.

_____ 1

(ii) The *Acacia* tree is adapted to withstand long periods of drought.

Suggest an adaptation the *Acacia* tree may show that allows it to survive long, dry periods.

_____ 1

(*b*) In Scottish grasslands, sheep are often found as grazers. A very large flock of sheep was introduced into an area of ungrazed grassland.

Explain why this would decrease biodiversity within this area.

_____

_____ 2

[Turn over

DO NOT
WRITE
THIS
MARGIN

Marks

9. The diagram below shows a section through a human heart.

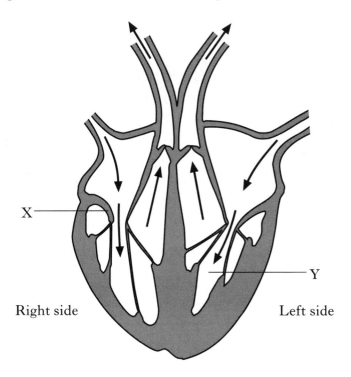

Right side   Left side

(a) Name valve X and chamber Y shown in the diagram.

X _____

Y _____   1

(b) Decide if each of the following statements about blood vessels is **True** or **False**, and tick (✓) the appropriate box.

If the statement is **False**, write the correct word in the **Correction** box to replace the word(s) underlined in the statement.

Statement	True	False	Correction
Capillaries contain valves.			
Veins allow gas exchange.			
Blood leaves the heart in arteries.			

3

Marks

9. **(continued)**

(*c*) The sentences below describe some of the functions of blood cells.

Underline one option in each set of brackets to make the sentences correct.

Oxygen is transported by $\left\{ \begin{array}{c} \text{red} \\ \text{white} \end{array} \right\}$ blood cells.

It combines with haemoglobin to form oxyhaemoglobin at $\left\{ \begin{array}{c} \text{low} \\ \text{high} \end{array} \right\}$ oxygen levels.

1

Antibodies are produced by $\left\{ \begin{array}{c} \text{macrophages} \\ \text{lymphocytes} \end{array} \right\}$

1

[Turn over

Marks

10. The chart below shows the temperature of a patient over a 5 day period. Readings were taken daily at 7am and 7pm.

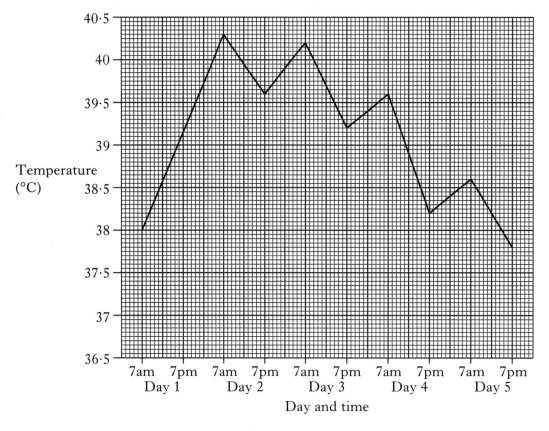

(*a*) (i) Calculate the temperature increase from 7am on Day 1 to 7am on Day 2.

Space for working

_____ °C   **1**

(ii) State **two** responses made by the body to cause the change in temperature observed on Day 2 from 7am to 7pm.

1. _____

2. _____   **2**

DO NOT WRITE IN THIS MARGIN

Marks

10. (continued)

(*b*) (i) Name the area of the brain containing the temperature regulating centre.

____________________ **1**

(ii) What term is used to describe the type of control mechanism which returns the body temperature to normal?

____________________ **1**

(iii) Describe how information is carried from temperature receptors in the skin to the brain.

____________________ **1**

[Turn over

Marks

11. The diagram below shows the human urinary system with its blood supply.

blood flow

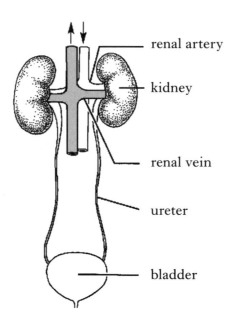

renal artery

kidney

renal vein

ureter

bladder

(a) An investigation was carried out to measure the concentration of three substances in samples of blood and urine.

The table below shows the results of this investigation.

Sample site	Concentration (grams per litre)		
	Glucose	*Urea*	*Salts*
Renal artery	1·0	0·3	8·0
Renal vein	0·8	0·0	6·0
Ureter	0·0	20·0	15·0

(i) Calculate the percentage of glucose remaining in the blood after it passes through the kidney.

Space for calculation

_____%   **1**

(ii) Explain how the data in the table supports the statement that urea is a waste product.

_____

_____   **1**

(iii) Name one substance, not shown in the table, which is present in urine.

_____   **1**

DO NOT WRITE IN THIS MARGIN

Marks

11. (continued)

(*b*) Name the two processes in the kidney which cause the differences in salt concentration between blood and urine.

Process 1 ______________________________ **1**

Process 2 ______________________________ **1**

(*c*) Freshwater bony fish use their kidneys to overcome a water balance problem.

Describe this problem and **one** method used by the kidneys to overcome it.

Problem ______________________________ **1**

Method ______________________________ **1**

[Turn over

Marks

12. (a) The diagram below shows the small intestine with associated organs and blood vessels.

Key: ⟶ direction of flow

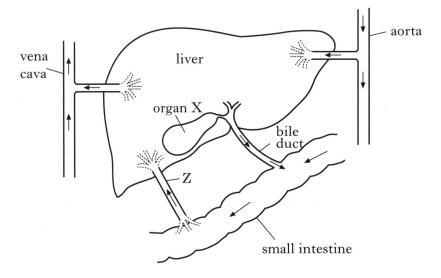

(i) Blood vessel Z carries amino acids to the liver.

(A) Name blood vessel Z.

_____ 1

(B) Describe what happens to excess amino acids in the liver.

_____ 1

(ii) (A) Name organ X.

_____ 1

(B) Describe the function of the bile that is released from organ X.

_____ 1

(b) Complete the table below which shows the substrate and product of two enzymes found in the small intestine.

Enzyme	Substrate	Product
	protein	
amylase		maltose

2

[Turn over for Section C on *page twenty-eight*

DO NOT
WRITE
THIS
MARGIN

Marks

SECTION C

Both questions in this section should be attempted.

Note that each question contains a choice.

**Questions 1 and 2 should be attempted on the blank pages which follow.
All answers must be written clearly and legibly in ink.**

Supplementary sheets, if required, may be obtained from the invigilator.

1.   Answer **either** A **or** B.

   A.   The diagram below shows a section through a flower.

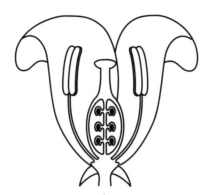

   Name the sites of production of pollen grains and ovules in a flower.
   Describe how these gametes are formed and describe the process of
   fertilisation.   5

   OR

   B.   The diagram below summarises a form of genetic engineering.

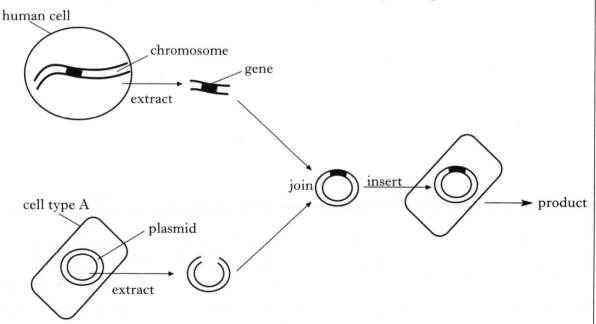

   Identify cell type A and name a product of genetic engineering.
   Describe the advantages and disadvantages of this process.   5

Question 2 is on *Page thirty*.

SPACE FOR ANSWER TO QUESTION 1

[Turn over for Question 2 on *Page thirty*

DO NOT WRITE IN THIS MARGIN

Marks

2. Answer **either** A **or** B.

Labelled diagrams may be included where appropriate.

A. Describe the function of yeast in bread making and the anaerobic pathway of respiration involved in this process. **5**

OR

B. Describe the properties of enzymes and the function of the enzyme phosphorylase in a synthesis reaction. **5**

[END OF QUESTION PAPER]

SPACE FOR ANSWER TO QUESTION 2

ADDITIONAL SPACE FOR ANSWERS

ADDITIONAL GRAPH PAPER FOR QUESTION 6(*a*)(i)

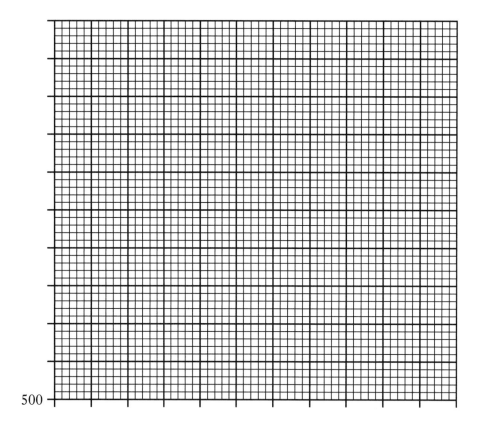

500

ADDITIONAL SPACE FOR ANSWERS

DO NOT
WRITE IN
THIS
MARGIN

ADDITIONAL SPACE FOR ANSWERS

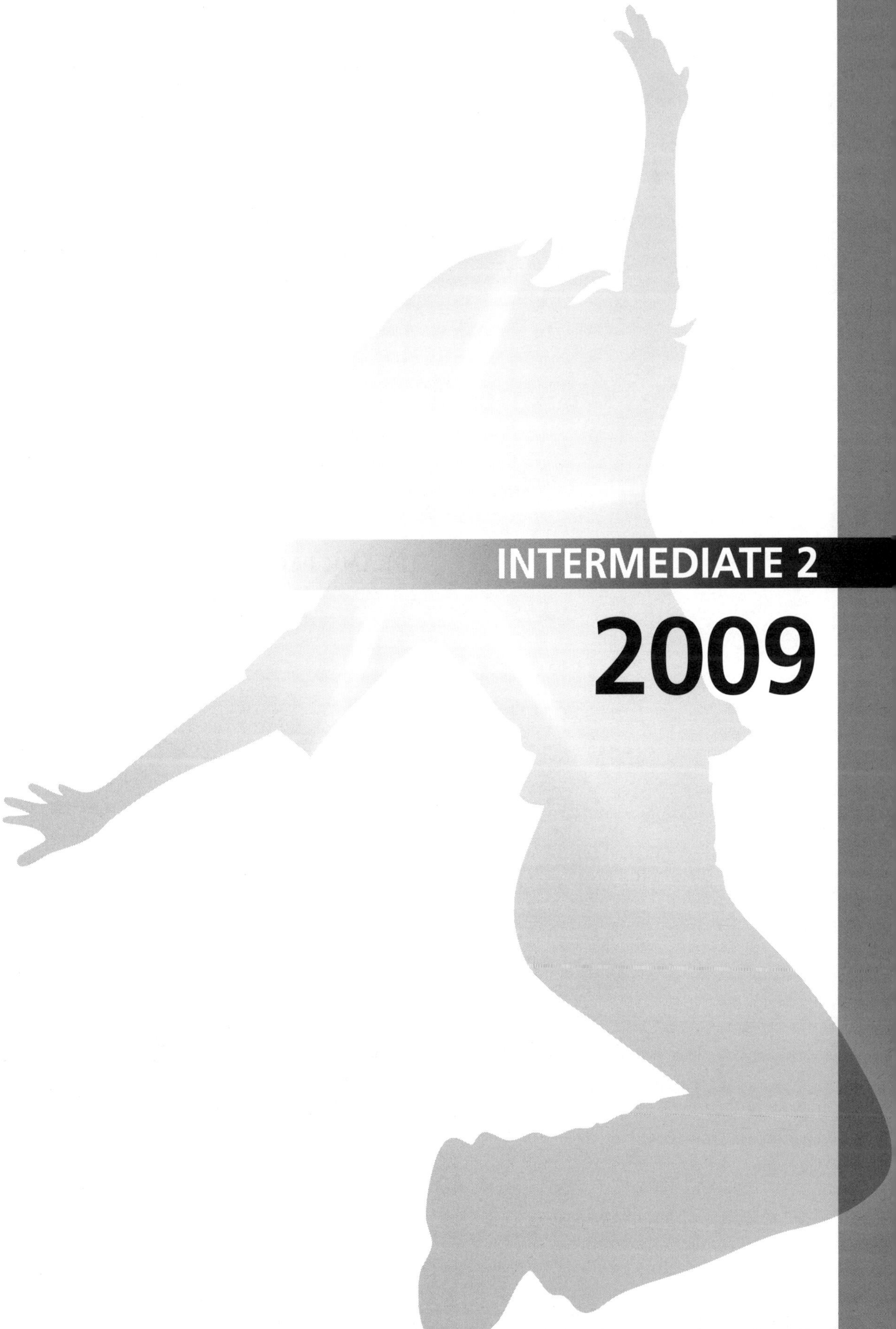

INTERMEDIATE 2

2009

[BLANK PAGE]

FOR OFFICIAL USE

Total for
Sections B and C

X007/201

NATIONAL
QUALIFICATIONS
2009

THURSDAY, 28 MAY
9.00 AM – 11.00 AM

BIOLOGY
INTERMEDIATE 2

Fill in these boxes and read what is printed below.

Full name of centre

Town

Forename(s)

Surname

Date of birth

Day　Month　Year

Scottish candidate number

Number of seat

SECTION A (25 marks)

Instructions for completion of Section A are given on page two.

For this section of the examination you must use an HB pencil.

SECTIONS B AND C (75 marks)

1　(a)　All questions should be attempted.

　(b)　It should be noted that in **Section C** questions 1 and 2 each contain a choice.

2　The questions may be answered in any order but all answers are to be written in the spaces provided in this answer book, **and must be written clearly and legibly in ink**.

3　Additional space for answers will be found at the end of the book. If further space is required, supplementary sheets may be obtained from the invigilator and should be inserted inside the **front** cover of this book.

4　The numbers of questions must be clearly inserted with any answers written in the additional space.

5　Rough work, if any should be necessary, should be written in this book and then scored through when the fair copy has been written. If further space is required, a supplementary sheet for rough work may be obtained from the invigilator.

6　Before leaving the examination room you must give this book to the invigilator. If you do not, you may lose all the marks for this paper.

Read carefully

1   Check that the answer sheet provided is for **Biology Intermediate 2 (Section A)**.

2   For this section of the examination you must use an **HB pencil** and, where necessary, an eraser.

3   Check that the answer sheet you have been given has **your name**, **date of birth**, **SCN** (Scottish Candidate Number) and **Centre Name** printed on it.

     Do not change any of these details.

4   If any of this information is wrong, tell the Invigilator immediately.

5   If this information is correct, **print** your name and seat number in the boxes provided.

6   The answer to each question is **either** A, B, C or D. Decide what your answer is, then, using your pencil, put a horizontal line in the space provided (see sample question below).

7   There is **only one correct** answer to each question.

8   Any rough working should be done on the question paper or the rough working sheet, **not** on your answer sheet.

9   At the end of the exam, put the **answer sheet for Section A inside the front cover of this answer book**.

Sample Question

Plants compete mainly for

A   water, light and soil nutrients

B   water, food and soil nutrients

C   light, water and food

D   light, food and soil nutrients.

The correct answer is **A**—water, light and soil nutrients. The answer **A** has been clearly marked in **pencil** with a horizontal line (see below).

Changing an answer

If you decide to change your answer, carefully erase your first answer and using your pencil, fill in the answer you want. The answer below has been changed to **D**.

SECTION A

All questions in this Section should be attempted.

1. The diagram below shows a cell.

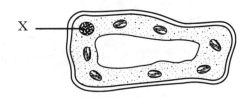

The function of structure X is to

A   control cell activities

B   keep the cell turgid

C   control entry and exit of material

D   release energy from glucose.

2. Fungi destroy bacteria by producing

A   antibiotics

B   alcohol

C   carbon dioxide

D   biogas.

3. The graph below shows the effect of temperature on the activity of the enzyme pepsin.

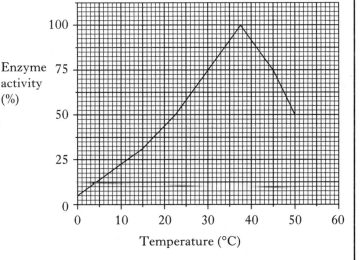

Between which two temperatures is there the greatest increase in enzyme activity?

A   0 – 10 °C

B   10 – 20 °C

C   20 – 30 °C

D   30 – 40 °C

4. In an investigation into the synthesis of starch from glucose-1-phosphate (G-1-P) by the enzyme phosphorylase, a tile was set up as shown below. Starch-free potato extract was used as the source of phosphorylase.

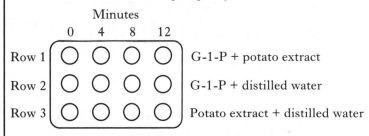

Iodine solution was added to the columns at the time intervals shown.

Which of the following tiles shows the expected result of this investigation?

[Turn over

5. An investigation was carried out to measure the rate of carbon dioxide production in bread dough.

Carbon dioxide production was measured by recording the change in volume of a sample of bread dough over a 50 minute period.

The results are shown in the table below.

Time (minutes)	0	10	20	30	40	50
Volume of dough (cm^3)	10	14	18	21	23	25

The conclusion for this investigation was

A $0.3 \, cm^3$ of carbon dioxide was produced per minute

B $0.5 \, cm^3$ of carbon dioxide was produced per minute

C $15 \, cm^3$ of carbon dioxide was produced per minute

D $25 \, cm^3$ of carbon dioxide was produced per minute.

6. The apparatus below was used to investigate respiration in germinating peas.

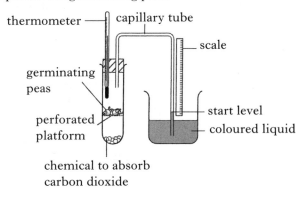

A suitable control for this investigation would be

A

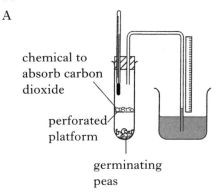

B

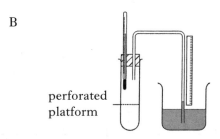

C

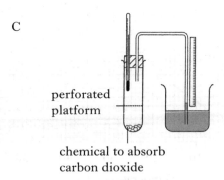

D

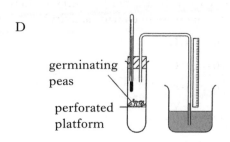

7. The graph shows the effect of varying the light intensity, temperature and carbon dioxide concentration on the rate of photosynthesis.

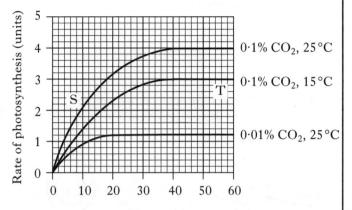

0·1% CO_2, 25 °C

0·1% CO_2, 15 °C

0·01% CO_2, 25 °C

The rate of photosynthesis is being limited by

A   temperature at S and light intensity at T

B   light intensity at S and temperature at T

C   carbon dioxide at S and temperature at T

D   light intensity at S and carbon dioxide at T.

8. Which of the following conditions in a greenhouse would produce earlier crops?

A   Glass shading

B   Cool air conditioners

C   Additional oxygen

D   Additional carbon dioxide

9. The diagram below shows part of a food chain in the Arctic tundra.

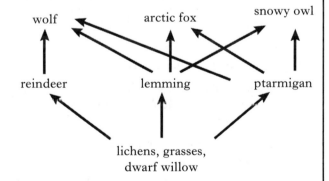

A population in this food web is all the

A   plants

B   reindeer

C   animals

D   living organisms.

10. The diagram below represents a field (Y) with an area (X) fenced off.

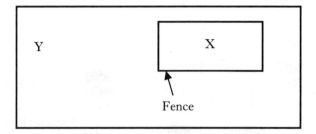

Sheep and rabbits provide very high intensity of grazing in area Y but cannot graze in fenced off area X.

Which line in the table below describes the diversity of plant species in areas X and Y after one year?

	Diversity of plant species	
	Area X	Area Y
A	higher	lower
B	lower	higher
C	higher	higher
D	lower	lower

11. The chromosome complement of a human individual who inherits an X-chromosome from their father is

A   44 including XX

B   44 including XY

C   46 including XX

D   46 including XY

[Turn over

12. In humans, the allele for free earlobes (E) is dominant to the allele for fixed earlobes (e).

The diagram below shows the inheritance of this characteristic.

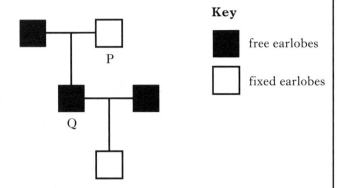

Key

■ free earlobes

□ fixed earlobes

Which line in the table identifies correctly the genotypes of persons P and Q?

	Genotype	
	P	Q
A	ee	EE
B	ee	Ee
C	EE	Ee
D	Ee	Ee

13. A hairy stemmed pea plant was crossed with a smooth stemmed pea plant and all of the F_1 had hairy stems.

The genotype of the hairy stemmed parent plant is

A heterozygous dominant

B heterozygous recessive

C homozygous recessive

D homozygous dominant.

14. In gerbils, agouti coat colour is dominant to white.

Some heterozygous gerbils were allowed to interbreed and 56 offspring were produced. What would be the expected number of agouti gerbils?

A 14

B 28

C 42

D 56

15. Skin colour in humans is an example of

A discontinuous variation

B co-dominance

C polygenic inheritance

D random assortment.

16. The diagram below shows stages in the production of a desired product by genetic engineering.

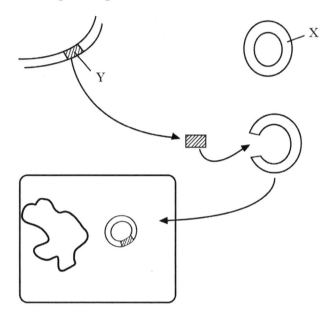

Which line in the table identifies correctly the structures labelled above?

	X	Y
A	bacterium	gene
B	plasmid	chromosome
C	bacterium	chromosome
D	plasmid	gene

17. Digestion takes place in animals

A and allows insoluble molecules to pass directly through the wall of the small intestine

B as enzymes cannot act on insoluble molecules

C and makes insoluble molecules into soluble molecules to allow absorption

D and allows food to be passed along the gut by peristalsis.

18. Salivary glands produce mucus to

A   lubricate the food in the stomach

B   lubricate the food to aid swallowing

C   protect the mouth from amylase

D   protect the oesophagus from amylase.

19. In the stomach, proteins are broken down into polypeptides.

The graph below shows the concentrations of protein and polypeptides in the stomach over 40 minutes.

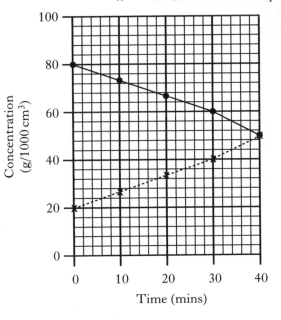

What was the ratio of protein concentration to polypeptide concentration after 30 minutes?

A   3 : 2

B   2 : 3

C   2 : 1

D   1 : 2

20. The diagram below shows some structures in a villus.

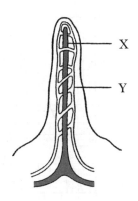

Which line in the table below correctly identifies the products of digestion which pass into structures X and Y?

	X	Y
A	glucose	amino acids
B	glycerol	fatty acids
C	amino acids	glycogen
D	fatty acids	glucose

21. Which line in the table identifies correctly the functions of the large intestine and the anus?

	Large intestine	Anus
A	digests food material	eliminates undigested material
B	stores undigested material	absorbs water from undigested material
C	absorbs water from undigested material	eliminates undigested material
D	absorbs digested food products	absorbs water from undigested material

22. The diagram below shows the human urinary system.

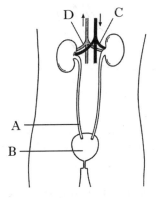

Which labelled part is the ureter?

23. The graph below shows the results of an investigation on the effect of ADH on urine production.

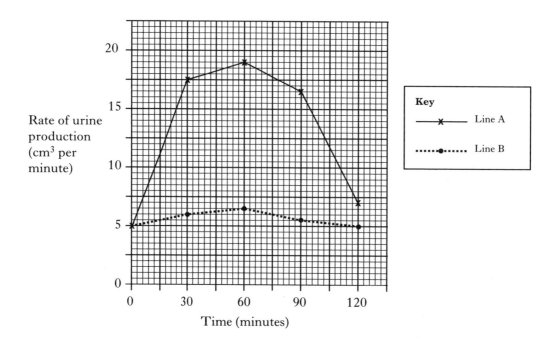

Line A shows the rate of urine production for a volunteer after drinking one litre of water.

Line B shows the rate of urine production from the same volunteer after drinking one litre of water and receiving an injection of ADH.

After 60 minutes, what was the difference between the rates of urine production with and without the ADH injection?

A   6·5 cm³ per minute

B   12·5 cm³ per minute

C   19·0 cm³ per minute

D   25·5 cm³ per minute

24. The diagram below shows an air sac with part of its capillary network.

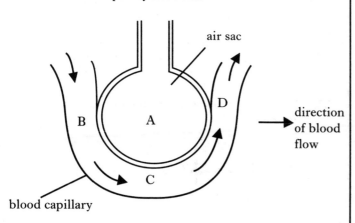

At which position would blood with the highest concentration of oxygen be found?

25. The diagram below shows a section through the human brain.

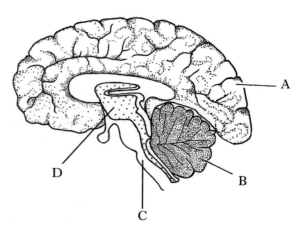

Which labelled part is the site of temperature regulation?

Candidates are reminded that the answer sheet for Section A MUST be placed INSIDE the front cover of this answer book.

SECTION B

All questions in this section should be attempted.
All answers must be written clearly and legibly in ink.

Marks

1. (*a*) The diagram below shows three stages X, Y and Z that occur when an enzyme converts its substrate into a product.

X   Y   Z

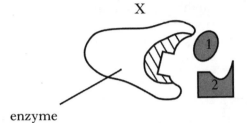 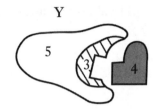 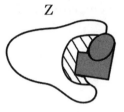

enzyme

     (i)   This enzyme promotes the breakdown of a complex molecule into simpler molecules.

        Put the stages into the correct order to show this degradation reaction.

        _____ ⟶ _____ ⟶ _____   1

     (ii) Which number in the diagram shows the active site?

        _____   1

  (*b*) Complete the following sentence by underlining the correct word from the choice in brackets.

Enzymes are made of $\left\{\begin{array}{l}\text{carbohydrate}\\\text{fat}\\\text{protein}\end{array}\right\}$.   1

  (*c*) Describe what happens to an enzyme when it is denatured.

_____

_____   1

[Turn over

Marks

2. Liver contains the enzyme catalase which carries out the following reaction.

   hydrogen peroxide ——➤ water + oxygen

The investigation shown below was carried out to demonstrate the effect of pH on catalase activity in liver.

Hydrogen peroxide of different pH values was added to 1 g of roughly chopped raw liver.

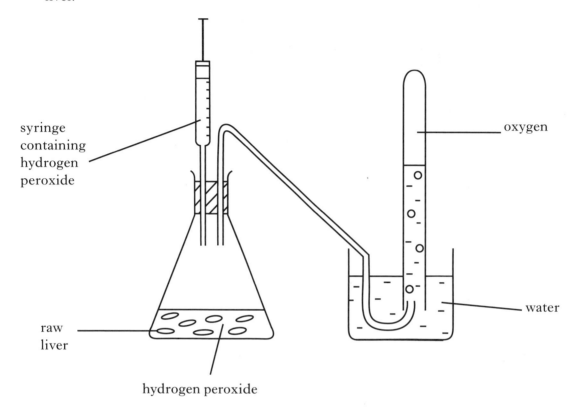

syringe containing hydrogen peroxide

oxygen

raw liver

water

hydrogen peroxide

The time taken to collect $1 cm^3$ of oxygen was recorded and the results are shown in the table below.

pH of hydrogen peroxide solution	Time to collect $1 cm^3$ of oxygen (seconds)			Average time to collect $1 cm^3$ of oxygen (seconds)
	Trial 1	Trial 2	Trial 3	
7	76	77	81	78
8	56	58	57	57
9	50	45	40	45
10	53	50	53	52
11	59	69	70	66

   (a) From the table, state the optimum pH for catalase in liver.

   _____

1

Marks

2. **(continued)**

(b) Name the variable altered in this investigation.

_____ **1**

(c) Explain why the experiment was repeated at each pH value and averages calculated.

_____ **1**

(d) Construct a line graph of the **average** time taken to collect $1 \, cm^3$ of oxygen against pH of hydrogen peroxide solution.

(Additional graph paper, if required, will be found on *Page thirty-two*)

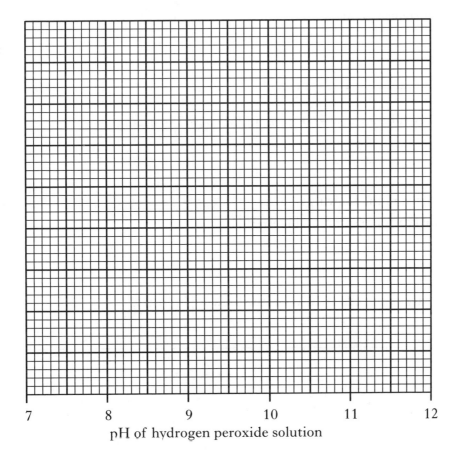

pH of hydrogen peroxide solution

2

(e) Predict the average time to collect $1 \, cm^3$ of oxygen at pH12.

_____seconds **1**

[Turn over

Marks

3. Yeast may carry out two different types of respiration.

   (a) Name the type of respiration in yeast which has the highest energy yield.

   _____

1

   (b) The diagram below shows one type of respiration in yeast cells.

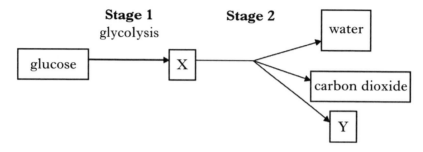

       (i) Name substances X and Y.

           X _____

1

           Y _____

1

       (ii) What other substance must be present for stage 2 to occur?

           _____

1

   (c) Yeast cells are used in the brewing industry.
       (i) Name the type of respiration involved.

           _____

1

       (ii) Explain why yeast cells are used in the brewing industry.

           _____

1

Marks

4. (*a*) The diagram below shows an investigation into the effect of adding three different solutions to three pieces of muscle tissue.

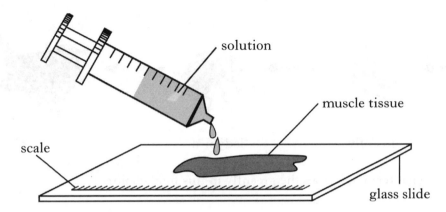

The results of the investigation are given in the table below.

Muscle tissue	Solution added	Length of muscle tissue			
		at start (mm)	*after 5 minutes* (mm)	*difference in length* (mm)	*percentage difference* (%)
1	1% glucose	50	50	0	0
2	1% ATP	45	41·5	4·5	10
3	0·5% ATP	48	45·6	2·4	

   (i) Calculate the percentage difference in length for muscle tissue 3.

    Space for calculation

                                                _____ %   1

   (ii) What conclusion can be drawn from the results?

    _____

    _____   1

(*b*)   (i) What term is used to describe the effect of lactic acid build up in muscle tissue?

    _____   1

   (ii) How can lactic acid be removed from muscle tissue?

    _____   1

Marks

5. (*a*) The diagram below represents a food chain in a garden.

(*The organisms are not to scale.*)

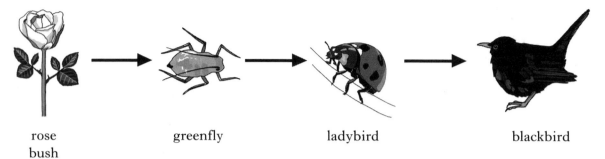

rose   greenfly   ladybird   blackbird
bush

(i) What term describes the greenfly in this food chain?

_____   1

(ii) A rose bush contains $10\,000\,kJ/m^2/year$ of energy and only 10% of this energy is passed on at each stage of the food chain.

Use this information to complete the pyramid of energy below for this food chain.

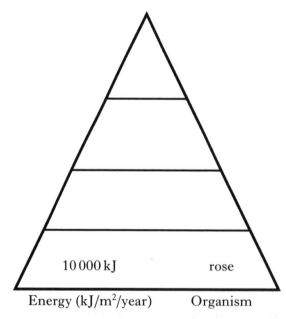

10 000 kJ   rose

Energy (kJ/m²/year)   Organism

2

(iii) What happens to the energy that is **not** passed on at each stage of the food chain?

_____   1

(*b*) Many ladybirds were seen over the summer in the garden.

They were able to interbreed and produce fertile offspring.

What can be concluded about the ladybirds, using all this information?

_____   1

Marks

6. The following table shows four blood groups and their frequency in a population.

Blood Group	Frequency in population (%)
O	44
A	42
B	10
AB	4

(a) Calculate the simplest whole number ratio of the frequency of blood groups O to AB.

Space for calculation

Blood group   _____ : _____
                 O   AB

1

(b) Name the type of variation shown by these blood groups.

_____

1

(c) Blood group is determined by three alleles A, B, O.

The table below shows the possible genotypes of each blood group.

Genotype	Blood group
OO	O
AO, AA	A
BO, BB	B
AB	AB

(i) Which of these alleles are co-dominant?

_____

1

(ii) Explain the meaning of co-dominant alleles.

_____

_____

1

Marks

7. (*a*) The diagram below shows a summary of events that occur during reproduction in a flowering plant.

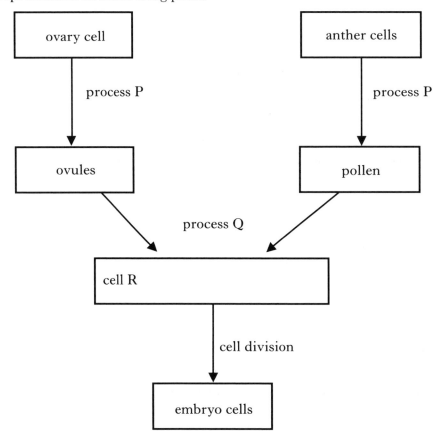

(i) **Complete the diagram** by entering the name of cell type R.   1

(ii) Which process in the diagram represents fertilisation?

_____   1

(iii) Complete the following table by inserting a tick (✓) in the correct boxes to show which of the cells in the diagram have a double or single set of chromosomes.

Cell	Double set of chromosomes	Single set of chromosomes
anther		
ovule		
R		
embryo		

2

Marks

7. **(continued)**

(b) Explain the need to produce cells with a single set of chromosomes in reproduction.

_____

_____　1

(c) <u>Underline</u> one option in each set of brackets to make the following sentence correct.

Random assortment of chromosomes occurs during $\left\{ \begin{array}{c} \text{meiosis} \\ \text{fertilisation} \end{array} \right\}$

which $\left\{ \begin{array}{c} \text{increases} \\ \text{decreases} \end{array} \right\}$ the $\left\{ \begin{array}{c} \text{biodiversity} \\ \text{variation} \end{array} \right\}$ of gametes.　2

[Turn over

Marks

DO NO
WRITE
THIS
MARGI

8. An investigation to demonstrate the responses of woodlice to light was carried out in a choice chamber. Half of the choice chamber was covered in black paper and the other half left in light.

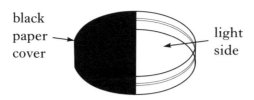

black
paper →
cover

light
side

Ten woodlice were introduced into the choice chamber. The number of woodlice in each side was counted every two minutes for ten minutes.

The graph shows the results of this investigation.

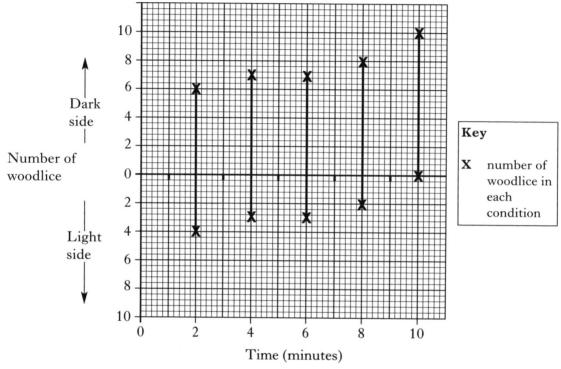

(a) Name two environmental conditions that should be kept constant in this investigation.

1 _____

2 _____ **2**

(b) What conclusion can be made from the results of this investigation?

_____

_____ **1**

(c) Explain the advantage of this behaviour to the woodlice.

_____

_____ **1**

Marks

9. It is thought that Darwin's finches evolved from one type of ancestral finch.

   The diagram below shows examples of different species of Darwin's finches.

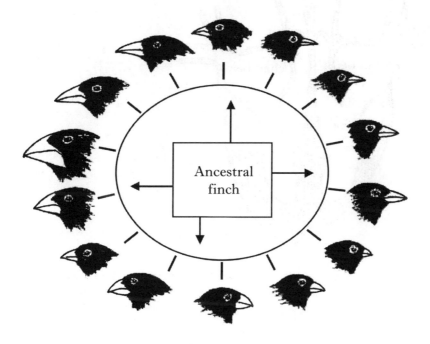

   (a) (i) What **two** observations can be made from the diagram about the structure of the finches' beaks?

   _____ 1

   (ii) Name one environmental factor which has led to this variation.

   _____ 1

   (b) What term is used to describe the role that each finch plays within its community?

   _____ 1

   (c) The existence of some Darwin's finches is under threat in the Galapagos Islands due to human activity.

   (i) Give an example of a human activity that could be affecting the finches.

   _____ 1

   (ii) What could be an effect of this human activity on finch biodiversity?

   _____ 1

[Turn over

Marks

10. The diagram below shows a section through the heart.

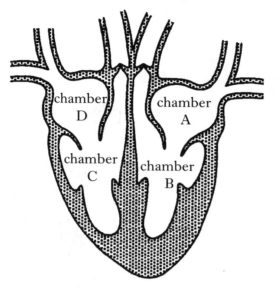

(a) (i) Blood follows a pathway through the heart and lungs from the vena cava to the aorta. Use letters from the diagram to complete the following flow chart to show the correct pathway.

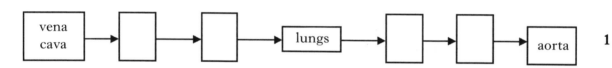

1

(ii) State the letter of a chamber of the heart which contains oxygenated blood.

Chamber _____

1

Marks

10. **(continued)**

(b) Decide if each of the following statements about the transport of gases by the bloodstream is **True** or **False**, and tick (✓) the appropriate box.

If the statement is **False** write the correct word in the **Correction box** to replace the word underlined in the statement.

Statement	True	False	Correction
Oxygen forms oxyhaemoglobin at <u>low</u> oxygen levels in the lungs.			
Carbon dioxide is transported in <u>red</u> blood cells.			
Carbon dioxide dissolved in the blood plasma <u>decreases</u> acidity.			

3

[Turn over

Marks

11. (*a*) An investigation was carried out to estimate the concentration of urea in two unknown urine samples. A tablet of the enzyme urease was added to a test tube containing the urine sample. When urease reacted with urea in the sample the gas produced turned moist litmus paper blue.

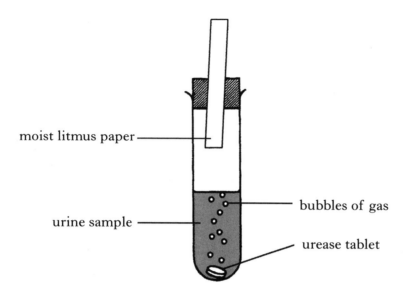

The time taken for the litmus paper to turn blue was recorded in each case.

The table below shows the results obtained when various urine samples of known and unknown urea concentration were tested.

Concentration of urea in urine sample (g/100 cm³)	Time taken for litmus paper to turn blue (seconds)
0·5	300
1·5	210
2·5	115
3·5	10
unknown A	75
unknown B	225

(i)   Which unknown urine sample, A or B, has the lowest concentration of urea?

_____   1

(ii) Suggest a reason for a low concentration of urea in urine.

_____   1

DO NOT WRITE IN THIS MARGIN

Marks

11. (*a*) (continued)

(iii) Predict the effect on the results if the temperature was increased from 20°C to 30°C in this investigation.

______________________________ **1**

(iv) Describe a suitable control for this investigation.

______________________________ **1**

(*b*) The diagram below shows the parts of a kidney nephron involved in filtration.

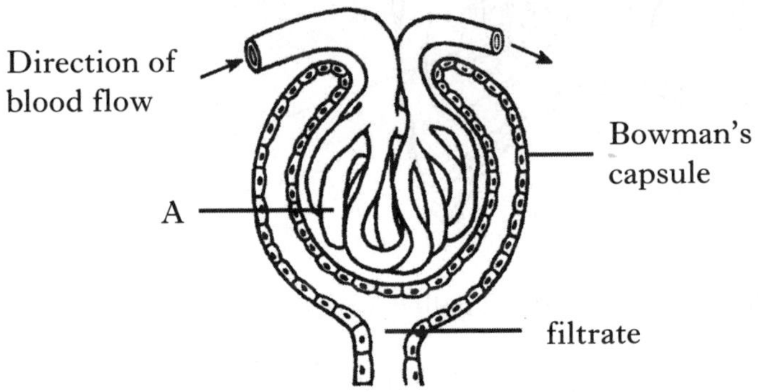

Direction of blood flow
Bowman's capsule
A
filtrate

(i) Name part A which consists of a bundle of blood capillaries.

______________________________ **1**

(ii) Describe the process which forms urine from the filtrate.

____

______________________________ **1**

[Turn over

Marks

12. (*a*) The diagram below shows the human breathing system.

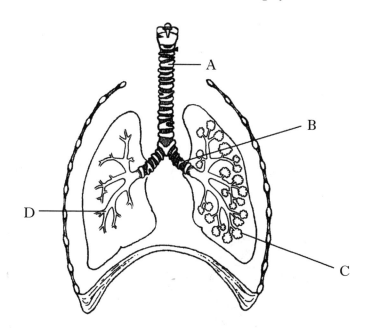

Complete the table below to identify the labelled structures.

Letter	Name of structure
	bronchiole
B	
	trachea
C	

2

Marks

12. **(continued)**

(*b*) A person breathed normally, took deep breaths, then returned to normal breathing.

The volume of air in the lungs was measured and the results are shown in the graph below.

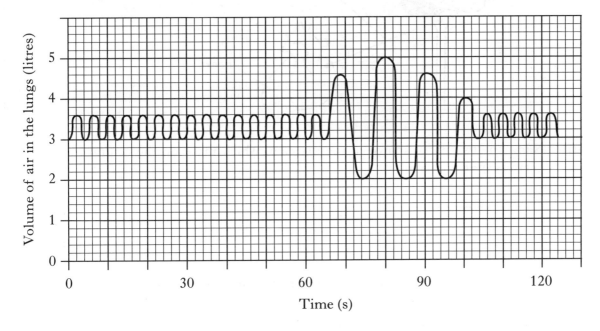

(i) What was the normal breathing rate for this person?

_____ breaths per minute   1

(ii) What was the highest volume of air inhaled in a single breath?

_____ litres   1

[Turn over

Marks

13. (*a*) The diagram below shows parts of the central nervous system (CNS) and a nerve to the heart.

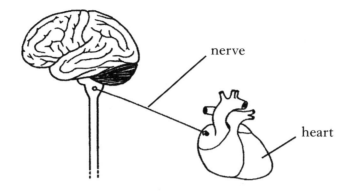

nerve

heart

(i) Name the two parts, shown in the diagram, which make up the central nervous system (CNS).

1 _____

2 _____   1

(ii) Name the area, shown in the diagram, which controls heart rate.

_____   1

(*b*) Reflex arcs contain relay fibres.

(i) Which structure sends impulses to the relay fibre?

_____   1

(ii) What is the function of relay fibres in a reflex arc?

_____   1

(*c*) Explain the function of a reflex response.

_____

_____   1

[Turn over for Section C on *page twenty-eight*

SECTION C

Both questions in this section should be attempted.

Note that each question contains a choice.

**Questions 1 and 2 should be attempted on the blank pages which follow.
All answers must be written clearly and legibly in ink.**

Supplementary sheets, if required, may be obtained from the invigilator.

Marks

1. Answer **either** A **or** B.

    A. The diagrams below show the two stages of photosynthesis.

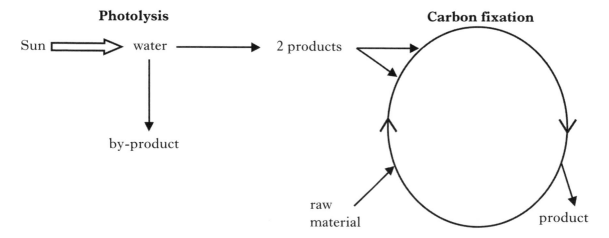

    Describe what happens during the two stages
    (*a*) photolysis

    and

    (*b*) carbon fixation.

5

OR

    B. The diagrams below show animal and plant cells in isotonic solutions.
        These diagrams are not to scale.

Animal cells	Plant cells
	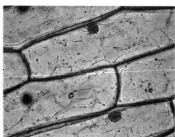

    Describe the osmotic effect of transferring

    (*a*) the animal cells into a hypotonic solution (water)

    (*b*) the plant cells into a hypertonic solution (strong salt).

5

Question 2 is on *Page thirty*

SPACE FOR ANSWER TO QUESTION 1

[Turn over for Question 2 on *Page thirty*

DO NOT WRITE IN THIS MARGIN

Marks

2. Answer **either** A **or** B.

Labelled diagrams may be included where appropriate.

A. Describe the role of the liver and pancreas in digestion. Include in your answer the processing of absorbed materials such as glucose and amino acids. **5**

OR

B. Describe the role of antibodies and phagocytosis in defence. Name the cells involved in each of these defence mechanisms. **5**

[*END OF QUESTION PAPER*]

SPACE FOR ANSWER TO QUESTION 2

ADDITIONAL SPACE FOR ANSWERS

ADDITIONAL GRAPH PAPER FOR QUESTION 2(*d*)

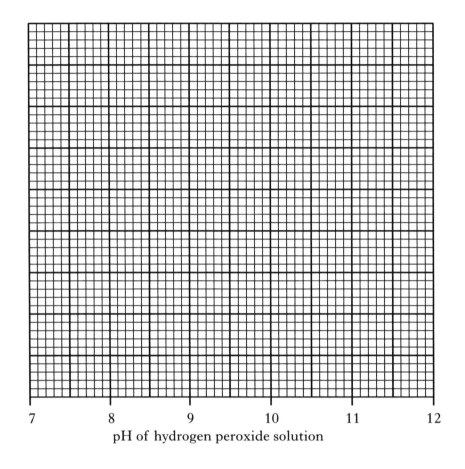

pH of hydrogen peroxide solution

ADDITIONAL SPACE FOR ANSWERS

ADDITIONAL SPACE FOR ANSWERS

[BLANK PAGE]

OFFICIAL SQA PAST PAPERS 149 INTERMEDIATE 2 BIOLOGY 2009

[BLANK PAGE]

[BLANK PAGE]

[BLANK PAGE]